The Abuse of Evil

The Abuse of Evil

The Corruption of Politics and Religion since 9/11

RICHARD J. BERNSTEIN

polity

First published in 2005 by Polity Press

Polity Press
65 Bridge Street
Cambridge CB2 1UR, UK.

Polity Press
350 Main Street
Malden, MA 02148, USA

ISBN: 0-7456-3493-1
ISBN: 0-7456-3494-X (pb)

A catalogue record for this book is available from the British Library.

Typeset in 10.5 on 12 pt Plantin
by Servis Filmsetting Ltd, Manchester
Printed and bound in the United States by the Maple Vail Book Manufacturing Group

The publisher has used its best endeavours to ensure that the URLs for external websites referred to in this book are correct and active at the time of going to press. However, the publisher has no responsibility for the websites and can make no guarantee that a site will remain live or that the content is or will remain appropriate.

Every effort has been made to trace all copyright holders, but if any have been inadvertently overlooked the publishers will be pleased to include any necessary credits in any subsequent reprint or edition.

For further information on Polity, visit our website: www.polity.co.uk

Contents

Could the activity of thinking as such, the habit of examining whatever happens to come to pass or attract attention, regardless of results and specific content, could this activity be among the conditions that make men abstain from evil-doing or even "condition" them against it?

Hannah Arendt, *The Life of the Mind*

Preface

On August 31, 2001, I completed the manuscript of my book, *Radical Evil*. Eleven days later, the most dramatic terrorist attack in history took place. No one now doubts that the world changed on that infamous day. Overnight (literally), we were bombarded with images and talk of evil. My book *Radical Evil* was an attempt to comprehend the horrendous evils experienced in the twentieth century. I wanted to see what we might learn about the meaning of evil from the modern philosophical tradition. I subtitled the book "A Philosophical Interrogation," and I interrogated Kant, Hegel, Schelling, Freud, Nietzsche, Levinas, Jonas, and Arendt in order to learn what they teach us about the nature of evil. I concluded the work with a series of theses. Here is my first thesis: "*Interrogating evil is an ongoing, open-ended process.* Throughout I have indicated my skepticism about the very idea of a theory of evil, if this is understood as a complete account of what evil is. I do not think that such a theory is possible, because we cannot anticipate what new forms of evil or vicissitudes of evil will appear." I did not realize, at the time, just how prophetic my claim would be.

After 9/11, I considered whether I wanted to revise my book, but I decided to let it stand as I had written it. Since 9/11, evil has become a popular, "hot" topic. Politicians, conservatives, preachers, and the media are all speaking about evil. Frankly, I have been extremely distressed by the post-9/11 "evil talk." I argue that the new discourse of good and evil, which divides the world according to this stark and simplistic dichotomy, is an *abuse of evil*. Traditionally, the discourse of evil in our religious, philosophical, and literary traditions has been intended to provoke *thinking*, questioning, and inquiry. But today, the appeal to evil is being used as a political tool to obscure complex issues, to block genuine thinking, and to stifle public discussion and debate. I argue that what we are now confronting is a *clash of mentalities*, not a clash of civilizations. A mentality that is drawn to absolutes, alleged moral certainties, and simplistic dichotomies stands in contrast to a mentality that questions the appeal to absolutes in politics, that argues that we must not confuse subjective moral *certitude* with objective moral *certainty*, and that is skeptical of an uncritical rigid dichotomy between the forces of evil and the forces of good. I call this mentality "pragmatic fallibilism." I also challenge what I consider to be the unjustified and outrageous claim that without an appeal to absolutes and fixed moral certainties we lack the grounds to act decisively in fighting our real enemies. There is no incompatibility between fallibilism and a passionate commitment to oppose injustice and immorality. I also argue that the post-9/11 abuse of evil *corrupts* both democratic politics and religion. There is no place for absolutes in democratic politics. And we violate what is most vital in the world religions when we uncritically assume that religious faith is a *sufficient* basis for knowing what is good and evil. There are religious and nonreligious fundamentalists and fanatics. And there are religious believers and nonreligious secularists whose beliefs, deeds, and emotions are informed by a robust fallibilism. The clash of mentalities cuts across the religious/secular divide.

The stakes are high in this clash of mentalities in shaping how we think and act in the world today – and in the future.

I want to thank John Thompson for encouraging me to write this book and Jean van Altena for her splendid editing. I also want to acknowledge my gratitude to Louis Menand and Farrar Straus Giroux for permission to cite passages from *The Metaphysical Club: A Story of Ideas in America.*

Introduction

Today our nation saw evil, the very worst of human nature.
George W. Bush, Address to the Nation,
September 11, 2001

America has shown its evil intentions and the proud Iraqi
people cannot accept it.
Moktada al-Sadr, April 7, 2004

What do we mean when we call an event, an intention, a
deed, or a human person evil? What are we referring to
when we use evil as a *noun*, when we say "Today our nation
saw *evil*." There is something chilling and powerfully emotional when we speak of evil. We feel that we know precisely
what we intend. There is no ambiguity or confusion about
what really is evil – even if we are at a loss to define what
we mean. And we also feel that there can be no compromise with evil. We must fight to eliminate it. When challenged to clarify what we mean by evil, we may appeal to
other expressions, such as unjust, immoral, wrong, sinful,
horrible, wicked, malevolent, sadistic, vicious, etc. But
none of these is as strong, terse, or compact as evil. To add
emphasis – to the name the worst – we speak of *absolute,
pure,* or *radical evil.* Although we sometimes compare evils
and use expressions such as "the lesser of two evils," more

often we think of evil in absolute terms. Evil is evil; there are no gradations here.

The concern with evil is as old as civilization itself. It is fundamental for all the major religions. Our greatest philosophers, theologians, poets, and novelists have struggled with the meaning and consequences of evil. It is a central theme in Plato, St Augustine, Shakespeare, Milton, and Dostoevsky. Theologians and philosophers speak of "the problem of evil," or the problem of "theodicy" – a word invented by the eighteenth-century philosopher Leibniz. If one believes that there is a God who is omniscient, omnipotent, and benevolent, then the question arises as to how we can reconcile the *appearance* of evil with the existence of such a God. The reason I stress *appearance* is because some thinkers have denied the *reality* of evil. Evil is a lack or privation of what is good; it lacks real existence. Others affirm the reality of evil, but claim that human beings, by misusing their free will, are responsible for the evil that exists in the world: free will, a gift from God, involves the *choice* of good or evil. Still others have challenged the idea that God is really omnipotent. If we survey the historical literature dealing with the "problem of evil," we find that almost every possibility has been explored which would reconcile the idea of a benevolent Creator with the existence of evil in this world. There are even some religious doctrines (considered to be heretical by Christianity) that deny the benevolence of the Deity. Actually, the traditional "problem of evil" is not concerned primarily with defining or characterizing the *meaning* of evil. Rather – whatever we take to be evil – the question is how we can reconcile the existence of evil with a belief in a loving God. The task is to "explain" or "justify" evil in a way that does not make God responsible for it. Sometimes, the problem of evil is used to challenge the existence of such a God. Dostoevsky's Ivan Karamazov argues passionately that the gratuitous murder of innocent children cannot be reconciled with a belief in a benevolent God.

Evil has been closely associated with suffering – especially suffering for which there does not seem to be any meaning or justification. This is why the Book of Job is frequently cited as one of the earliest discussions of how the apparent evil of Job's suffering can be reconciled with faith in a just God. It would be a serious mistake to think that the "problem of evil" is exclusively a religious problem. Secular thinkers have raised similar questions. They too want to know how to make sense of a world in which evil seems to be so intractable. Nietzsche declared that human beings do not repudiate suffering as such: it is *meaningless* suffering that is so intolerable. And the French philosopher Emmanuel Levinas has argued that *any* attempt (religious or secular) to *justify* or rationalize the horror of evil is a form of theodicy; we must resist the *temptation* of theodicy.

At the beginning of the modern age, many thinkers classified evils as either natural or moral. Natural evils are those that occur without *direct* human intervention. Perhaps the most famous example was the devastating Lisbon earthquake that struck the city on the morning of November 1, 1755, and buried thousands of persons in the rubble. The question – debated throughout Europe – was whether such a terrible event was compatible with a faith in the Christian God. What kind of God would allow the death of so many innocent people? The best minds in Europe, including Voltaire, Rousseau, and Kant, struggled with the question. And it caught the popular imagination in pamphlets and sermons of the time. Today, most of us do not think of such terrible natural events as earthquakes, tsunamis, tornadoes, and hurricanes as manifestations of evil. The entire category of natural evils has been called into question, in part because of what Max Weber calls the "disenchantment of nature." Susan Neiman claims that the Lisbon earthquake marked the birth of modernity because "it demanded recognition that nature and morality are split" (Neiman 2004: 267).

The discourse about evil in the twentieth century has been extremely paradoxical. There are some philosophers and theologians who have continued to struggle with the classic problem of evil. But these discussions have become specialized and esoteric; they are remote from the concerns of everyday life. Moral philosophers tend to focus on what is just and unjust, right and wrong, moral and immoral. Kant, who many think of as the greatest of modern moral philosophers, argued that the *justification* of moral claims ought to be independent of our religious beliefs. We may learn our morality – our sense of what is right and wrong, good and bad – from our religious upbringing, but this does not mean that the *justification* of our morality is based on religious beliefs. Even those moral philosophers who disagree sharply with Kant's claims about the foundations of morality generally accept the claim that morality should be clearly distinguished from religion.[1] Consequently, many moral philosophers have avoided discussing evil, because evil is so intimately tied to religious discourse.

But at the same time, ever since we have become aware of the full horrors of the Nazi period and the perverse cruelty of the Shoah, Auschwitz has come to symbolize the most extreme evil of our time – an evil unprecedented in history. Hannah Arendt is one of the very few thinkers who sought to comprehend what is distinctive about the new form of evil that burst forth with twentieth-century totalitarianism. Appropriating Kant's expression *radical evil*, she tells us:

> Evil has proved to be more radical than expected. In object-
> ive terms, modern crimes are not provided for in the Ten
> Commandments. Or: the Western Tradition is suffering

from the preconception that the most evil things human beings can do arise from the vice of selfishness. Yet we know that the greatest evils or radical evil has nothing to do any more with such humanly understandable, sinful motives. (Arendt and Jaspers 1992: 166)

But what is radical evil? Radical evil is making human beings superfluous as human beings. This happens as soon as all unpredictability – which, in human beings, is equivalent to spontaneity – is eliminated. We can understand more fully what she means by turning to the description she gives of total domination. She presents a three-stage model of the "logic" of total domination. It is in the concentration and death camps that we find the "laboratories" of totalitarian regimes. And it is in the camps that we find the most radical experiments for changing the character of human beings.

"The first essential step on the road to total domination is to kill the juridical person in man" (Arendt 1968: 447). This started long before the Nazis established the death camps. Arendt is referring to the legal restrictions that stripped Jews (and other groups such as homosexuals and gypsies) of their juridical rights. "The aim of an arbitrary system is to destroy the civil rights of the whole population, who ultimately become just as outlawed in their own country as the stateless and the homeless. The destruction of man's rights, the killing of the juridical person in him, is a perquisite for dominating him entirely" (Arendt 1968: 451). Inmates in concentration camps have no rights.

"The next decisive step in the preparation of living corpses is the murder of the moral person in man. This is done by making martyrdom, for the first time in history, impossible" (Arendt 1968: 451). The SS, who supervised the camps, were perversely brilliant in corrupting all forms

of human solidarity. They succeeded in making questions
of conscience questionable and equivocal.

> When a man is faced with the alternative of betraying
> and thus murdering his friends or of sending his wife
> and children, for whom he is in every sense responsible, to
> their death; and when even suicide would mean the imme-
> diate murder of his own family, how is he to decide? The
> alternative is no longer between good and evil, but between
> murder and murder. Who could solve the moral dilemma
> of the Greek mother, who was allowed by the Nazis to
> choose which of her three children should be killed? (Arendt
> 1968: 452)

But this is not yet the worst. There is a third step on the
road to total domination – and it is here that we come face
to face with the core of radical evil.

> After the murder of the moral person and annihilation of the
> juridical person, the destruction of individuality is almost
> always successful … For to destroy individuality is to
> destroy spontaneity, man's power to begin something new
> out of his own resources, something that cannot be
> explained on the basis of reactions to environment and
> events. (Arendt 1968: 455)

The camps served the ghastly experiment of eliminating,
under scientifically controlled conditions, spontaneity
itself as an expression of human behavior and of trans-
forming the human personality into a mere thing. There
was a systematic attempt to transform human beings into
"living corpses," to fabricate human beings who were not
quite human – who were at once human and inhuman.
This is what Arendt takes to be the quintessence of radical
evil; this is what she means by making human beings as
human beings superfluous. Arendt is referring to those

living corpses who were called *Muselmann* – so graphically described by Primo Levi, a survivor of Auschwitz.

> Their life is short, but their number is endless; they the *Muselmänner*, the drowned, they form the backbone of the camp, an anonymous mass, continually renewed and always identical, of non-men who march and labor in silence, the divine spark dead in them, already too empty to really suffer. One hesitates to call them living: one hesitates to call their death death, in the face of which they have no fear, as they are too tired to understand.
>
> *They crowd my memory with their faceless presence, and if I could enclose all the evil of our time in one image, I would choose this image which is familiar to me: an emaciated man, with head dropped and shoulders curved, on whose face and in whose eyes not a trace of thought is to be seen.* (Levi 1986: 90, emphasis added)[2]

When Arendt described radical evil in *The Origins of Totalitarianism*, she focused on describing the phenomenon – the systematic transformation of human beings into something less than fully human. She didn't explicitly explore the motivations of the Nazi perpetrators, although she did speak of the absolutely cold and systematic destruction of human bodies. This was the clear intention of those who administered the camps. But the question of motives and intentions became much more problematic for her when she reported on the trial of Adolph Eichmann. Arendt called into question one of our most central and entrenched moral and legal convictions: namely, that people who do evil deeds must have evil motives and intentions. They are vicious, sadistic, or wicked. She claimed that Eichmann was not a sadistic monster. He was "terrifyingly normal"; he was "a new type of criminal who commits his crimes in circumstances that make it well-nigh impossible to know or feel that he is doing wrong"

(Arendt 1965: 276). His *deeds* were monstrous, and he deserved to hang, but his motives and intentions were banal. One of the clearest statements of what Arendt means by the "banality of evil" is in her 1971 lecture "Thinking and Moral Considerations."

> Some years ago, reporting the trial of Eichmann in Jerusalem, I spoke of the "banality of evil" and meant with this no theory or doctrine but something quite factual, the phenomenon of evil deeds, committed on a gigantic scale, which could not be traced to any particularity of wicked-ness, pathology, or ideological conviction in the doer, whose only personal distinction was perhaps extraordinary shallowness. However monstrous the deeds were, the doer was neither monstrous nor demonic, and the only specific characteristic one could detect in his past as well as in his behavior during the trial and the preceding police exam-ination was something entirely negative: it was not stupidity but a curious, quite authentic inability to think. (Arendt 1971: 417)

Susan Neiman sums up why *Eichmann in Jerusalem* makes such an important contribution to understanding evil in our time – and why it is still so controversial.

Auschwitz embodied evil that confuted two centuries of modern assumptions about intention.

Those assumptions identify evil and evil intention so thoroughly that denying the latter is normally viewed as a way of denying the former. Where evil intention is absent, we may hold agents liable for the wrongs they inflict, but we view them as matters of criminal negligence. Alternatively, anyone who denies that criminal intention is present in a particular action is thought to exonerate the criminal. This is the source of the furor that still surrounds Arendt's *Eichmann in Jerusalem*, the twentieth century's most import-ant philosophical contribution to the problem of evil.

The conviction that guilt requires malice and forethought led most readers to conclude that Arendt denied guilt because she denied malice and forethought – though she often repeated that Eichmann was guilty, and was convinced that he ought to hang. Her main point is that Eichmann's harmless intentions did *not* mitigate his responsibility. (Neiman 2004: 271–2)

Historians have raised many questions about the factual accuracy of Arendt's portrait of Eichmann, but this does not diminish the significance of her main point – that normal people with banal motives and intentions can commit horrendous crimes and do evil deeds.[3] But despite the lack of evil intentions, they are fully responsible for their acts. Furthermore, Arendt's warning is as relevant for us today as it was when she wrote it: "The sad truth of the matter is that most evil is done by people who never made up their minds to be or to do either evil or good" (Arendt 1977b: 180).

Auschwitz has come to epitomize the evil of the Nazi regime. But, unfortunately, it is only one of the *many* genocides that have occurred in the twentieth century – and continue to take place in the twenty-first century. Despite such slogans as "Never Again," genocides continue to break out in different parts of the world. Each one is distinctive in its circumstances, methods, and character, but each brings forth new manifestations of evil. There is a protean quality about evil. It changes its shape and takes on ever new forms. This is why it is so difficult to define or characterize. What is so frightening is that once some new evil is introduced, it sets a precedent for what may happen again.

When we survey historical attempts to comprehend evil, there is one characteristic that stands out. The confrontation with evil provokes *thinking*. St Augustine draws on all his imaginative, emotional, and intellectual powers to reconcile the appearance of evil with his firm belief in a loving God. Leibniz thought we needed a new discipline – theodicy – to explain *rationally* why everything happens for the best. Shakespeare explores the intricacies of the moral psychology of evil in such characters as Iago, Lady Macbeth, and Richard III. No one poses the questions about evil more brilliantly than the characters in Dostoevsky's novels. And Hannah Arendt returned over and over again to confront anew the evils of the twentieth century.

But something different happened on 9/11. Overnight (literally) our politicians and the media were broadcasting about evil. We were flooded with headlines about evil and images displaying evil – from the repetitive TV images of the crumbling of the towers of the World Trade Center to the smirking faces of Osama bin Laden and Saddam Hussein. Suddenly the world was divided in a simple (and simplistic) duality – the evil ones seeking to destroy us and those committed to the war against evil. There have been other times in recent history when politicians – especially in the United States – have used the rhetoric of good and evil to gain support from their constituencies. Ronald Reagan called the Soviet Union "The Evil Empire." But, despite this rhetoric, Reagan was flexible and pragmatic in his diplomatic negotiations when Gorbachev became the leader of the Kremlin. What is so disturbing about the post-9/11 evil talk is its rigidity and popular appeal. Few stop to ask what we really mean by evil. What are we saying when we label our enemies "evil"? And who precisely are our enemies? It is presumably self-evident. In a world where there is fear and anxiety about unpredictable threats of terrorism that can strike at any place and any time, it is psychologically reassuring to label the enemy "evil."

I want to examine this new fashionable popularity of the discourse of good and evil. I will argue that it represents an *abuse* of evil – a dangerous abuse. It is an abuse because, instead of inviting us to question and to *think*, this talk of evil is being used to stifle *thinking*. This is extremely dangerous in a complex and precarious world. The new discourse of good and evil lacks nuance, subtlety, and judicious discrimination. In the so-called "War on Terror," nuance and subtlety are (mis) taken as signs of wavering, weakness, and indecision. But if we think that politics requires judgment, artful diplomacy, and judicious discrimination, then this talk about absolute evil is profoundly *anti-political*. As Hannah Arendt noted, "The absolute . . . spells doom to everyone when it is introduced into the political realm" (Arendt 1963: 79). Our proclamations about evil and the "axis of evil" are matched by fanatical talk of a jihad committed to eliminating evil infidels. Consider the statement that I cited as my second epigraph to this introduction. If we substitute the phrase "Moktada al-Sadr and his militant cohorts" for "America," and "the proud American people" for "the proud Iraqi people," then we have the type of statement that we hear so frequently from Washington. "Moktada al-Sadr and his militant cohorts have shown their *evil* intentions and the proud American people cannot accept it."

Before 9/11 many fundamentalists and conservative Christian evangelicals exhibited restraint in condemning Islam. But since 9/11 this has changed. Franklin Graham, Billy Graham's son and heir to his ministry, declared that Islam is a "wicked and evil religion." This is the type of inflammatory rhetoric that is matched by the diatribes of Islamic fundamentalists against Christianity and Judaism as evil religions.

Samantha Power succinctly and eloquently describes the contrast between more thoughtful responses to evil and the new stark opposition of black (evil) and white (good) in her recent comment about Hannah Arendt.

Arendt used the phrase "radical evil" to describe totalitarianism, and this idea has been brought back in circulation. Yet while Arendt did not allow such branding to deter her from exploring the sources of that evil, the less subtle minds who invoke the concept today do so to mute criticisms of their responses. (Who, after all, can be against combating evil?)

But sheltering behind black-and-white characterizations is not only questionable for moral or epistemological reasons. It poses a practical problem because it blinds us from understanding and thus undermines our long-term ability to prevent and surmount what we don't know and most fear. "Evil," whether radical or banal, is met most often with unimaginativeness. Terrorism is a threat that demands a complex and elaborate effort to distinguish the sympathizers from the militants and to keep its converts to a minimum. Terrorism also requires understanding how our past policies helped give rise to such venomous grievances. (Power 2004: 37)

We need to probe the mentality that neatly divides the world into the forces of evil and the forces of good, to understand its sources and its appeal. For this is an outlook that is currently widespread in American culture, from Hollywood to Washington, although it has a much longer history, reaching back to ancient forms of Gnosticism and Manichaeism. It stands in sharp opposition to another mentality that is more open and fallible, and has a robust sense of the unpredictability of contingencies – an outlook that demands questioning and inquiry along with firm resistance to concrete evils. I want to expose and challenge the claim frequently made by those who find simple stark contrasts and oppositions so appealing. The champions of the new "evil" discourse claim that the only alternative to such a firm and clear understanding of good and evil is a wishy-washy (secular) relativism that lacks the serious commitment to oppose and eliminate evil. This is the way in which many neo-conservatives characterize their political opponents. They are weak and vacillating; they lack the moral conviction, realism, firmness, and fervor to do what is required to fight and eliminate evil. We are told that if we give up on "moral certainties," we will lack the backbone to fight our enemies. Nietzsche spoke about the desire for "metaphysical comfort." He meant the smugness and self-righteousness – the false sense of security – that arises when we *delude* ourselves into thinking that we have firm and absolutely *certain* foundations for our moral convictions. But we can (and must) learn to live without "metaphysical comfort," to live with a realistic sense of unpredictable contingencies – and at the same time to have a passionate commitment to understand, resist, and fight concrete evils and oppose injustices. Questioning the new superficial discourse of good and evil requires digging into the foundations of what is rarely critically examined – the dualistic outlook that underlies this mentality. It also requires questioning one of the most pernicious assumptions made by the champions of the new discourse. This is the assumption that firm moral convictions and actions rest upon moral certainties and absolutes.

Let me clarify what I will criticize. We frequently appeal to "certainty" in perfectly legitimate ways. If I am asked whether I saw John yesterday, I may reply that "I am absolutely certain that I saw him." But if I discover that John was actually in another city yesterday, I do not hesitate to admit that I was mistaken. "Certainty" is used to express our *certitude*, our subjective personal conviction that something is so-and-so. But all too frequently there is a slide from this subjective sense of *certitude* to an objective sense of certainty – where we act as if the *strength* of our personal conviction is sufficient to justify the objective *truth* of what we are claiming. *Subjective certitude or personal*

conviction by itself is never sufficient to justify objective truth.
The mentality that I will be criticizing is one that thinks
that affirming one's certitude and the depth of one's sincere
conviction is sufficient to justify the claim of objective
certainty.

There are also appeals to absolutes that may be perfectly
legitimate. Many religious believers will appeal to God as
their absolute. But it is always appropriate to ask what the
person of faith means thereby. What is her *understanding* of
what she calls the absolute? Once we realize that any appeal
to an absolute requires *understanding* and *interpretation,*
then there is an opening for critical reflection on the truth
and adequacy of one's claims. We enter what Wilfrid
Sellars has called the "logical space of reasons," of asking
for and giving reasons – and this may include *religious*
reasons. But there are those who refuse to enter this space.
They do not think that any further justification, discussion,
or understanding is necessary. To put the point in a slightly
more technical way, I am denying that there are any *self-
authenticating epistemological* episodes – episodes where the
mere *having* of such episodes yields genuine knowledge.
This is what Sellars calls "the myth of the given" (Sellars
1963: 140).

Finally, when I challenge a rigid dualistic mentality –
one that divides the world into the "forces of good" and the
dark "forces of evil" – I am not calling into question the
importance of making sharp distinctions. We cannot think
or act in the world without doing so. At times, we do need
to make a clear distinction between friends and enemies.
But there is a danger that distinctions become reified and
rigid in ways that obscure complex issues. This is what has
happened with the popular post-9/11 dichotomy of good
and evil. I agree with *The 9/11 Commission Report* when it
asserts: "But the enemy is not just 'terrorism,' some generic
evil. This vagueness blurs the strategy. The catastrophic

threat at this moment in history is more specific. It is the threat of Islamist terrorism – especially the Al-Qaeda network, its affiliates, and its ideology" (p. 362). In short, I intend to criticize the *uncritical* or *unreflective* appeal to objective certainty, absolutes, and rigid dualisms.

We also need to explore the relation of this new discourse of good and evil to politics and religion. I have already suggested that it is anti-political. The appeal to absolutes is disastrous for politics. But there are also questions about religion and morality. The popular discourse about good and evil – especially in the United States – is permeated with an aura of religious piety. It is commonly believed that the justification for dividing the world into good and evil is supported by fundamental (Christian) religious beliefs. Almighty God is invoked as the source and justification for firm moral convictions. There is also a disparity and a dissonance between the philosophical understandings of morality and the widespread popular view. Philosophers may tell us that when it comes to matters of justification, our morality – our sense of what is right and wrong, or good and bad – is autonomous. We do not need to appeal to religion to justify or warrant moral beliefs. They may tell us that the great achievement of (Western) modernity has been to distinguish morality from religion. But this is not the prevailing view of many religious believers. They believe that it is their religion that is the source and justification for their morality. The Bible tells us that God gave the Ten Commandments to Moses on Mount Sinai. In the West, religion generally means the Judaic-Christian tradition. But, of course, Muslims believe that Allah is the source of all morality. When they speak of a holy war, or jihad, it is a religious war against evil infidels justified by God.

Does it make sense to speak of *the* Christian, Judaic, or Muslim conception of good and evil? Many believers who invoke God or Allah do *not* think that there is any ambiguity and uncertainty about this. I will argue that there is no *single religious* conception of good and evil. And further-more, that there is no *univocal* Christian, Judaic, or Muslim conception of good and evil. Stated positively, living reli-gious traditions are rich, complex, and always undergoing historical transformation. They contain different, compet-ing, conflicting, and even contradictory historical concep-tions of good and evil. Thus, for example, Christians today condemn the Spanish Inquisition's "religious" justification of torture. We now condemn this as a perversion of "authentic" Christianity – as being thoroughly *unchristian*. Indeed, Pope John Paul II explicitly condemned torture as an *intrinsic evil*. We distort and do violence to religious trad-itions when we fail to appreciate their changing historical character. Consequently, we must be wary and extremely skeptical about any form of religious reification or *essential-ism*. When we examine the world religions, we find that there are competing conceptions of good and evil that are *internal* to these traditions. We should be critical of those who appeal to their religious beliefs as if they provided unambiguous and univocal justification for their moral certainties. This does not mean that the world religions lack moral content. But it does mean that interpretation and questioning of religious doctrines is always required. In a living religious tradition, there is always a conflict of inter-pretations. I want to show that when we unmask the current popular discourse of good and evil, which is saturated in religious language, it turns out to be *anti-religious*. It violates what is best and most vital in the living world religions.

The battle that I see taking place is not between religious believers with firm moral commitments and secular rela-tivists who lack conviction. It is a battle that cuts across the so-called religious/secular divide. It is a battle between those who find rigid moral absolutes appealing, those who think that nuance and subtlety mask indecisiveness, those who embellish their ideological prejudices with the language of religious piety, and those who approach life with a more open, fallibilistic mentality – one that eschews the quest for absolute certainty. Such a mentality is not only compatible with a religious orientation; it is essential to keeping a religious tradition alive and relevant to new situations and contingencies. What we are confronting today is *not* a clash of civilizations, but a *clash of mentalities*. And the outcome of this clash has significant *practical* consequences for how we live our everyday lives – for our morality, politics, and religion.

1

The Clash of Mentalities

The Craving for Absolutes versus Pragmatic Fallibilism

In the Introduction I spoke about the clash of mentalities. In this chapter I want to explain what I mean, and why I think this clash is so consequential. By a mentality, I mean a general orientation – a cast of mind or way of thinking – that conditions the way in which we approach, understand, and act in the world. It shapes and is shaped by our intellectual, practical, and emotional lives. Mentalities can take a variety of concrete historical forms. We never encounter a mentality in the abstract, but only in a particular historical manifestation. To fully understand a specific historical manifestation of a mentality, we need to locate its context, its distinctive character, and its sources. We need to pay careful attention to its historical particularity – although we can recognize its similarities (and differences) with other historical examples of the same or similar mentalities. Mentalities also arise at different stages in history – and their concrete manifestations can pass away. So we also need to inquire about why they arise at a certain time and why they fade away. I want to begin with a specific historical example, one that has had a great influence on the character of the United States in the late nineteenth century and the first part of the twentieth century. After examining this important example of what I call pragmatic fallibilism, I will then, in the next chapter, reflect on its more general significance – and its relevance to our current situation.

Several years ago, Louis Menand published a fascinating book, *The Metaphysical Club: A Story of Ideas in America*. It explores the intellectual history of American pragmatism and seeks to situate this movement in the context of American history. (The Metaphysical Club was an informal discussion group of intellectuals who met in Cambridge, Massachusetts, during the 1870s to discuss philosophical issues.) Pragmatism as a philosophical movement arose in the United States just after the Civil War. This was a time when the idea of a research university – modeled on the German university – began to take hold throughout the United States. Before the Civil War, most private institutions of higher learning were colleges founded by different religious groups. The primary purpose of these colleges was to educate citizens and clergy rather than to engage in research. But during the latter part of the nineteenth century, there was a flourishing of independent scholarship in the natural sciences, social disciplines, and humanities. It was during this period that American thinkers sought do develop a distinctive philosophical orientation.

William James first popularized the expression "pragmatism" in a famous address that he delivered at the University of California, Berkeley, in 1898. In his address, "Philosophical Conceptions and Practical Results," James generously acknowledged his debt to Charles S. Peirce, "one of the most original contemporary thinkers," and James refers to "the principle of practicalism – or pragmatism as he called it when I first heard him enunciate it at Cambridge in the early '70s" (James 1977: 348). James first heard Peirce discuss his pragmatic principle at meetings of the Metaphysical Club. James introduces "Peirce's principle" with a metaphorical description: "the soul and meaning of thought, he says, can never be made to direct itself towards anything but the production of belief, belief being the demicadence which closes a musical phrase in the symphony of our intellectual life." James tells us that "beliefs, in short are really rules of action; and the whole function of thinking is but one step in the production of habits of action" (James 1977: 348). In 1898, Peirce was barely known as a philosopher (except to a small group of admirers such as James). Peirce, the son of a famous Harvard mathematician, was a scientist and a logician, but his intellectual curiosity spanned the entire range of human disciplines. As James's popular version of pragmatism spread, Peirce was so appalled and outraged that he renamed his own doctrine of meaning " 'pragmaticism' which is ugly enough to be safe from kidnappers" (Peirce 1931–5: 5. 414). There is a famous quip that pragmatism is the movement that was founded on James's misunderstanding of Peirce. Peirce and James were lifelong friends – although at times their friendship was a stormy one. Another young member of the Cambridge circle who joined the discussions of the Metaphysical Club was Oliver Wendell Holmes, Jr., who later became one of the most famous justices of the United States Supreme Court. John Dewey, born in 1859 (the year of publication of Darwin's *Origin of Species*), was 20 years younger than James. He came from a background that was very different from that of Cambridge intellectuals. He was born in Burlington, Vermont, the son of a shopkeeper, and was educated at the University of Vermont. Dewey was among the first American philosophers to get a Ph.D. degree at the newly founded graduate school, Johns Hopkins University. Peirce briefly taught at Johns Hopkins when Dewey was a graduate student. When Dewey joined the faculty of the University of Chicago in 1890, he was already a great admirer of James. Dewey claimed that James's magnum opus, *The Principles of Psychology*, had an enormous influence on his own intellectual development. And James himself was enthusiastic about the philosophical orientation being developed by the "Chicago School" centered on Dewey. In one of Dewey's most important books, *Experience and Nature*, Dewey praised Holmes as "one of our greatest philosophers," and quoted a long passage from Holmes's essay on "Natural Law." Holmes admired *Experience and Nature* – a book that shared his own conception of experience and existence. With his typical charming wit, Holmes wrote: "Although Dewey's book is incredibly ill written, it seemed to me ... to have a feeling of intimacy with the universe that I found unequaled. So methought God would have spoken had He been inarticulate but keenly desirous to tell you how it was" (quoted in Menand 2001: 437).

One of Menand's major contributions was to show how the origins of the pragmatic movement could be understood as a *critical response* to the horrors and excesses of the Civil War – the war that split the nation. Menand focused attention on four persons, Oliver Wendell Holmes, Jr., William James, Charles S. Peirce, and John Dewey, although he also discussed many of their contemporaries. Menand made a bold claim about the influence of these four men. He declared:

Their ideas changed the way Americans thought – and continue to think – about education, democracy, liberty, justice, and tolerance. And as a consequence they changed the way Americans live – the way they learn, the way they express their views, the way in which they understand themselves, and the way in which they treat people who are different from them. We are still living, to a great extent, in a country these thinkers helped to make. (Menand 2001: p. xi)

What is the bond that unites these very diverse thinkers? Menand affirms that they shared a common attitude toward ideas.

> What was that attitude? If we strain out the differences, personal and philosophical, they had with one another, we can say that what these four thinkers had in common was not a group of ideas, but a single idea – an idea about ideas. They all believed that ideas are not "out there" waiting to be discovered, but are tools . . . that people devise to cope with the world in which they find themselves. They believed that ideas are produced not by individuals, but by groups of individuals – that ideas are social. They believed that ideas do not develop according to some inner logic of their own, but are entirely dependent, like germs, on their human careers and environment. And they believed that since ideas are provisional responses to particular situations, their survival depends not on their immutability but on their adaptability. (Menand 2001: p. xi)

This "single idea" did not develop in an intellectual vacuum. It emerged in response to the violent extremism of the American Civil War. These thinkers were reacting against the entrenched opposition, the absolute certainty by the opposing forces of the righteousness of their cause, the sheer intolerance toward those who held opposing convictions – an intolerance that frequently set members of the same family against each other. This rigid mentality led to bloody violence. It was a mentality in which there were stark oppositions, a black-and-white world in which there was no possibility of compromise or negotiation. Holmes fought in the Civil War and was seriously wounded several times. James had a brother who nearly died in the war. Dewey was a young child during the war, but his father fought in the war. (Peirce, however, dreaded the draft. Through his father's influence, he secured a position in the

US Coastal Survey and managed to avoid conscription.) But the consciousness of the Civil War shaped an entire generation. Menand's thesis is that the pragmatic thinkers undertook to develop a more flexible, open, experimental, and fallible way of thinking that would avoid all forms of absolutism, stark binary oppositions, and violent extremism. And in their individual and collective way of doing this, they helped to reshape the ways in which Americans thought and acted.

I believe that Menand is essentially correct in the way in which he approaches the historical situatedness of the pragmatic movement. We tend to think that philosophers are somehow completely divorced from history – as if they were simply engaged in a timeless conversation with each other across the centuries. There have been philosophers who have characterized philosophy in this manner, but the pragmatic thinkers rejected this ahistorical conception of philosophy. Dewey, for example, always maintained that philosophy is (and ought to be) responsive to the deepest conflicts of its own time. Menand has written the type of intellectual history that reflects Dewey's own understanding of the cultural rootedness of philosophical speculation, and he presents a far more dramatic and vivid understanding of role played by this movement in reshaping the mentality of American life. There is another virtue in Menand's approach. He helps us to see that when the pragmatists critically attacked absolutism, when they sought to expose the quest for certainty, when they argued for an open universe in which chance and contingency are irreducible, they were not concerned exclusively with abstract metaphysical and epistemological issues. They were addressing profound ethical, political, and practical questions that ordinary people confront in their everyday lives. They were haunted by the memory of the way in which the conflict of absolutes led to so much bloody violence. They wanted to develop a new way of thinking – a new mentality – that would be an alternative to, and would overcome, all forms of entrenched ideological extremism.

In all the pragmatic thinkers there is a sustained multifaceted attack on what Dewey called "the quest for certainty." It is not just ideologists and fanatics who claim to live by absolute certainty. Dewey thought that this quest had been one of the most basic goals of the Western philosophical tradition. Dewey related this quest for certainty to a quest for *security*, an attempt to flee from the contingency, uncertainty, and ambivalence of everyday life. Many traditional philosophers had tended to valorize what is eternal, fixed, unchanging, and necessary, and to denigrate what is changing, becoming, contingent, and perilous. But there is no "escape from peril," from the vicissitudes of existence. Furthermore, we are neither playthings of forces that are always operating behind our backs; nor can we ever completely control our destinies. Dewey, like the other pragmatic thinkers, sought to expose the arrogance of those who think that they can anticipate, manipulate, and control all unexpected contingencies. All the pragmatists rejected doctrines of mechanical determinism that allow no place for genuine human agency and freedom. But they were just as relentless in their critiques of gratuitous voluntarism – the belief that we can initiate significant changes in the world simply by willing them. The important pragmatic task is to develop those ideas – and even more important – those flexible critical habits and practices that will enable us to cope with what is unexpected and unpredictable in a reflective intelligent manner.

Dewey coined the phrase "the spectator theory of knowledge." He argued that many traditional and modern philosophers were dominated by ocular metaphors, and that they tended to approach knowing as a form of passive seeing, or contemplation. Integral to the change in mentality that he and the other pragmatists sought to develop was the intellectual experiment of situating human beings as *agents*, not as passive spectators – agents who are always already undergoing and shaping their experience in transactions with their world. Dewey, like the other pragmatists, was skeptical of radical utopian "solutions," and he was suspicious of the idea of *total* revolution. But he was committed to ongoing radical social reform. Throughout his long life, his central concern was the character and fate of democracy. He felt that the greatest threats to American democracy were internal ones – threats in which the public was being manipulated by powerful special interest groups. He was concerned about "the eclipse of the public" – the eclipse of an informed public where there is open communication, debate, and deliberation. Dewey warned about the threat to democracy that resulted from the growth and spread of the "corporate mentality" – a mentality that has taken on global dimensions in our time.

> The business mind, having its own conversation and language, its own interests, its own intimate groupings in which men of this mind, in their collective capacity, determine the tone of society at large as well as the government of industrial society. . . . We now have, although without formal or legal status, a mental and moral corporateness for which history affords no parallel. (Dewey 1930: 41)

Democracy, according to Dewey, does not consist exclusively of a set of institutions, formal voting procedures, or even legal guarantee of rights. These are important, but they require a culture of everyday democratic cooperative *practices* to give them life and meaning. Otherwise institutions and procedures are in danger of becoming hollow and meaningless. Democracy is "a way of life," an ethical ideal that demands *active* and *constant* attention. And if we fail to work at creating and re-creating democracy, there is no guarantee that it will survive. Democracy involves a reflect-ive faith in the capacity of all human beings for intelligent judgment, deliberation, and action if the proper social, educational, and economic conditions are furnished. When Dewey was celebrating his eightieth birthday he pre-sented a talk entitled "Creative Democracy – The Task Before Us," in which he outlined his vision of a true demo-cratic society:

> Democracy as compared with other ways of life is the sole way of living which believes wholeheartedly in the process of experience as end and as means ... and which releases emotions, needs, and desires so as to call into being the things that have not existed in the past. For every way of life that fails in its democracy limits the contacts, the exchanges, the communications, the interactions by which experience is steadied while it is enlarged and enriched. The task of this release and enrichment is one that has to be carried on day by day. Since it is one that can have no end till experience itself comes to an end, the task of democracy is forever that of creation of a freer and more humane experience in which all share and to which all contribute. (Dewey 1988: 229–30)

Dewey understood that at times of deep uncertainty, anxiety, and fear, there is a craving for moral certainty and absolutes. At such times there can be a desperate search for metaphysical and religious comfort. But this is precisely what we must *resist*. For such comfort is based on illusions. Furthermore, as Peirce had already emphasized, such an appeal to absolutes blocks the road to open inquiry and genuine thinking. The pragmatists exposed and sharply attacked the seductive but misleading appeal to absolutes, certainty, specious foundations, and simplistic oppositions. But their main positive achievement was to develop a viable critical and fallible alternative.

Hilary Putnam, a leading contemporary philosopher who strongly identifies with the pragmatic tradition, claims that pragmatism is a "way of thinking" that involves "a certain group of theses, theses which can and indeed were argued very differently by different philosophers with different concerns." He summarizes these key theses as

> (1) antiskepticism; pragmatists hold that doubt requires justification just as much as belief . . .; (2) fallibilism; pragmatists hold that there is never a metaphysical guarantee to be had that such and such a belief will never need revision (that one can be fallibilistic and antiskeptical is perhaps the unique insight of American pragmatism); (3) the thesis that there is no fundamental dichotomy between "facts" and "values"; and the thesis that, in a certain sense, practice is primary in philosophy. (Putnam 1994: 152)

Peirce consistently challenged the idea of epistemological and metaphysical foundationalism that he took to be so basic for many philosophers – the dream or nightmare of discovering once and for all an incorrigible foundation that could serve as a basis for building the edifice of knowledge. There are deep philosophical, religious, social, and psychological reasons for this search for solid foundations and incorrigible truths. Descartes, more than any other thinker, vividly portrayed what he took to be the grand Either/Or that we confront: *Either* solid foundations and indubitable knowledge *Or* a swamp of unfounded and ungrounded opinion. I once called this "the Cartesian Anxiety" (Bernstein 1983: 16–24). Descartes' search for an Archimedean point is much more than a device to solve metaphysical and epistemological problems. It is the quest for some fixed ground, some stable rock upon which we can secure our lives against the vicissitudes that constantly threaten us. The specter that hovers in the background of the journey of the soul that Descartes undertakes in his

Meditations is the dread of chaos and madness where nothing is fixed and determinate, where – to use his own chilling metaphor – we are in a sea where we can neither touch bottom nor support ourselves on the surface. This anxiety has haunted intellectual and popular thinking right up to the present. It can take many different forms. And indeed, I believe that those today who claim religious or moral certainty for dividing the world into the forces of good and the forces of evil are shaped by this Cartesian Anxiety. For they are *claiming* the type of certainty for their moral and political convictions that Descartes claimed for his indubitable foundation. They also make use of the grand Either/Or when they attack their opponents. For they claim that the only alternative to solid foundations and moral certainties is to be lost in a quagmire of relativistic opinions.

Now what is distinctive about the pragmatic thinkers is that they rejected this grand Either/Or. The exclusive disjunction: "absolute" certainty *or* "absolute" relativism is specious. We need to *exorcize* the Cartesian Anxiety, or, to switch metaphors, engage in a form of philosophical therapy that will release us from its constraining grip. Beginning with Peirce, the pragmatists sought to develop the idea of fallibilism as a genuine alternative to the Cartesian Either/Or. Fallibilism is the belief that any knowledge claim or, more generally, any validity claim – including moral and political claims – is open to ongoing examination, modification, and critique. Peirce originally argued that fallibilism is essential for understanding the distinctive character of modern experimental science. Scientific inquiry does not have any absolute epistemological starting-points or end-points. Inquiry is a *self-corrective enterprise* that – in the words of Wilfrid Sellars – "can put any claim in jeopardy, though not *all* at once" (Sellars 1997: 79). The phrase "though not *all* at once" is crucial, because we could not even engage in any inquiry unless we *take* some claims and beliefs to be basic and unquestioned. But the key word here is "take" because further inquiry may teach us that what we have *taken* to be basic may need to be questioned and revised. Consequently, there is an uncontroversial sense in which we start from foundations and "takens." These are beliefs and "truths" that we take for granted in order to conduct an inquiry. These are warranted claims that have been established by previous inquiries. In the course of the self-corrective process of inquiry, these may also be questioned, revised, and even abandoned. And the self-corrective process of inquiry requires a *critical community of inquirers*. Peirce extended this notion of self-corrective inquiry to philosophy itself. But it was James, and especially Dewey, who sought to show the full significance of fallibilism for moral, social, and political inquiry in a democratic society. And Holmes's approach to the law is pervaded by a fallibilistic ethos that eschews all forms of absolute principles. In the *Common Law*, Holmes declared, "The life of the law has not been logic; it has been experience"(quoted in Menand 2001: 341).

Fallibilism, in its robust sense, is not a rarified epistemological doctrine. It consists of a set of virtues – a set of practices – that need to be carefully nurtured in critical communities. A fallibilistic orientation requires a genuine willingness to test one's ideas in public, and to listen carefully to those who criticize them. It requires the imagination to formulate new hypotheses and conjectures, and to subject them to rigorous public testing and critique by the community of inquirers. Fallibilism requires a high tolerance for uncertainty, and the courage to revise, modify, and abandon our most cherished beliefs when they have been refuted. Robust fallibilism requires what Karl Popper (who was influenced by Peirce) called the "open society." Consequently, fallibilism involves more than a minimal tolerance of those who differ from us and challenge our ideas. We must confront and seek to answer their criticisms and objections – and this requires mutual respect.

This fallibilistic mentality helps us to appreciate what Putnam means when he ascribes to the pragmatists "the thesis that there is no fundamental dichotomy between 'facts' and 'values'; and the thesis that, in a certain sense, practice is primary in philosophy."[1] To reject the idea of a fundamental *dichotomy* between "facts" and "values" is *not* to reject the idea that there are facts – and that objective facts are all important in any inquiry. Rather, Putnam seeks to emphasize the ways in which our interests and values shape what we *take* to be the facts in a given context. Furthermore, a fallibilistic mentality becomes meaningful and effective only when it becomes concrete in our every-day practices.

The pragmatists knew how difficult it is to cultivate and sustain a fallibilistic mentality. It does not come into being simply by talking about it or willing it. Fallibilism becomes a concrete reality only if we succeed in developing the proper critical habits and practices in a democratic society. This is an ongoing task that is never completed. Dewey's lifelong interest in education, especially in the education of the young, was motivated by his conviction about the importance of the role of the schools in nurturing a falli-bilistic mentality.

We can now better understand what Putnam means when he underscores the pragmatic insight that one can be fallibilistic and anti-skeptical. When Putnam speaks of skepticism, he is referring to the philosophical doctrine that calls into question the very *possibility* of knowledge. But fallibilism is not skepticism in this sense. It does not raise skeptical doubts about the very possibility of know-ledge. On the contrary, it is intended to bring out the essential characteristics of what constitutes legitimate knowledge – including both common sense and scientific knowledge. But fallibilism does raise doubts about the very possibility of *absolute incorrigible knowledge*. The pragmatists are not saying that the idea of such absolute knowledge is a desirable goal, but that we finite human beings can never achieve it. They are making a much more forceful and challenging claim: *the very idea of absolute incorrigible knowledge is incoherent.* Consequently, fallibilism does not lead to despair about the possibility of gaining knowledge, but seeks to illuminate how we can secure warranted knowledge claims and make progress in our inquiries.

In contrast to the philosophical doctrine of epistemological skepticism, there is a more commonsense concept of "skepticism," such that we can even speak of fallibilistic skepticism. Menand succinctly describes the liberating quality of the fallibilistic skepticism advocated by the pragmatic thinkers.

> The belief that ideas should never become ideologies – either justifying the status quo, or dictating some transcendent imperative for renouncing it – was the essence of what they taught.
>
> In many ways this was a liberating attitude, and it accounts for the popularity of Holmes, James, and Dewey (Peirce was a special case) enjoyed in their lifetimes, and for the effect they had on a whole generation of judges, teachers, journalists, philosophers, psychologists, social scientists, law professors, and even poets. They taught a kind of skepticism that helped people cope with life in a heterogeneous, industrialized, mass-market society, a society in which older human bonds of custom and community seemed to have become attenuated, and to have been replaced by more impersonal networks of obligation and authority. ... Holmes, James, Peirce and Dewey helped to free thought from the thralldom to official ideologies, of the church or the state or even the academy. There is also, though, implicit in

what they wrote, a recognition of the limits of what thought can do in the struggle to increase human happiness. (Menand 2001: p. xii)

There is another motif that is characteristic of a pragmatic fallibilistic mentality. William James was the first philosopher to dignify the word "pluralism" when he entitled one of his last books *A Pluralistic Universe*. There is no single system, no single all-encompassing philosophy, that stands for all time. The universe is pluralistic, and we as finite agents have multiple and limited perspectives in coping with this universe. He argued that philosophers frequently tend to substitute their rarified neat abstractions for the thick tangled plurality of life itself. Few philosophers have equaled James in his ability to describe, elicit, and celebrate the concrete plurality and varieties of human life.

The pragmatists also anticipated the importance of what has become the overwhelming fact of contemporary life: the plurality of cultural, ethnic, and religious differences. When James delivered his Oxford lectures in 1908, which were later published as *A Pluralistic Universe*, two young Americans were in the audience: Horace Kallen, a Jewish American, and Alain Locke, the first African American to be a Rhodes scholar. They had already formed a friendship during their student days at Harvard. Both were deeply influenced by James's vision of pluralism, and sought to apply James's ideas to articulating the notion of "cultural pluralism." Horace Kallen coined the expression "cultural pluralism." And Kallen's own defense of cultural pluralism led to a lively discussion among many who had been shaped by the pragmatic mentality, including Alain Locke, W. E. B. Du Bois (another student of James), and Randolph Bourne. Because anti-Semitism and racism were so prevalent in the United States at the time, there was a strong *practical* motivation in the pragmatic effort to develop a viable conception of cultural pluralism. The pragmatic thinkers advanced "cultural pluralism" as a norm and an ideal when there was an outbreak of xenophobia in the United States. In the 1920s Congress passed extremely restrictive immigration laws to keep out "undesirable foreigners." These laws were "justified" by pseudo-scientific appeals to eugenics, in order to keep America "racially pure."[2] Once again, the pragmatists found themselves fighting a pernicious absolute mentality – one that divided the world into "we Americans" and "undesirable foreigners."

Because there are not only different shifting individual and group identities but also conflicting and clashing ones, the problem of the tolerance of differences has become especially acute in contemporary life. We live at a time when there are powerful tendencies toward globalization. But this globalization increases our awareness of heterogeneity and differences. Throughout the world tensions and hostilities flare up among different cultural, religious, and ethnic groups. During the past 50 years many thinkers have been acutely aware of the significance of difference, otherness, alterity, and incommensurability. There is something extremely important in this new consciousness, but also something that is excessive and disturbing. There is a legitimate reaction to what James calls "intellectualism," and to what is sometimes called "abstract universalism," a type of universalism that is insensitive to particularity and pluralism. Ethnic, cultural, and religious groups who feel that their very identity is threatened in the name of some presumably universal ideal have strongly resisted assimilation. These so-called universal ideals turn out – so it is claimed – to mask the prejudices of a dominant and powerful group. In the name of "openness" and "tolerance," there is a disguised intolerance. We expect others to be and to act just like us, and we expect them to adopt and accept our norms and values. Emmanuel

Levinas is right when he claims that there has been a deep tendency in Western thought to try to assimilate the "other" to the "same" – to obliterate the singularity of the otherness of the other. He speaks of this tendency as "ontological imperialism," and when he does so, he is not using a dead metaphor. For the same logic is at work in political, economic, and cultural imperialism.

But we must also be alert to the *excessive* celebration of difference, otherness, and alterity. Not all forms of difference are desirable or to be welcomed. Some of these we must strongly oppose – especially those that seek to undermine or eliminate genuine plurality. Consequently, we need to develop a *critical* fallibilistic attitude toward cultural differences, distinguishing those that are to be welcomed and embraced in a pluralistic society from those that threaten the very existence of such a society. And here too, I believe that a pragmatic mentality is helpful in overcoming the specious dichotomy between abstract universalism and an uncritical celebration of singularity and difference. Although the pragmatists emphasize plurality, difference, and otherness, they were never guilty of what Karl Popper once called "the myth of the framework." This is the myth that we are prisoners caught in the framework of our own theories, cultures, values, and language – so much so that we cannot communicate with those who are encased in "radically" different, incommensurable frameworks. The "myth of the framework" leads straight to the type of relativism that undermines the *critical* evaluation of plural cultural practices. The pragmatists consistently advocated an *engaged pluralism* – an orientation wherein we acknowledge what is different from us, but seek to understand and critically engage it.[3]

In opposition to the myth of the framework, which treats different cultures and languages as if they were completely closed and self-contained, the pragmatists argued that it is always possible to move beyond and enlarge our limited horizon. We do this through the dialogical encounter with what is other and different. Failure to engage with what is strange and alien is a *practical* failure, a failure of imagination, and a failure to make an effort to understand what is different from us. *Pluralism is not relativism.* As a corollary to Putnam's claim that the pragmatists elaborated a fallibilism that is anti-skeptical, I would add that they also developed a pluralism that is anti-relativistic. Engaged pluralism is the very opposite of relativism. It demands that we make a serious effort to really understand what is other and different from us. It requires that we engage in the *critique* of our own views as well as those of the people we encounter.

To complete this portrait of the mentality of pragmatic fallibilism, I want to explore one final theme that is necessary for grasping its essential character. This is the centrality of the notions of chance and contingency. Peirce introduced a positive conception of chance. During his lifetime – before the discovery of quantum physics – many philosophers and scientists accepted some version of mechanistic determinism that left no room for chance. Presumably, the laws of nature are such that everything that ever happens is completely fixed according to these laws. From this perspective, "chance" is just a name for our ignorance of these laws. If we had full knowledge of these laws, then we would see that what appears to be a chance event is really fully determined. The French scientist Pierre-Simon Laplace, who declared that "we must ... imagine the present state of the universe as the effect of its prior state and the cause of the state that will follow it," put forth one of the most famous statements of this philosophy of determinism.

An intelligence which, for a given instant, could know all the forces by which nature is animated, and the respective situation of the beings who compose it, if, moreover, it was sufficiently vast to submit these data to analysis, if it could embrace in the same formula the movements of the greatest bodies in the universe as well as those of the lightest atom – nothing would be uncertain for it, and the future, like the past, would be present to its eyes. (Quoted in Menand 2001: 196)

Peirce argued that this notion of determinism was neither a presupposition nor a warranted conclusion of actual scientific inquiry. It is an unwarranted a priori *prejudice* – one that is completely unjustified by the actual practice of experimental science. Indeed, Peirce argued that actual scientific laws are not absolutely precise and determinate. As Menand tells us:

> If scientific laws are not absolutely precise, then scientific terminology has to be understood in a new way. Words like "cause" and "effect," "certainty" and "chance," even "hard" and "soft" cannot be understood as naming fixed and discrete entities or properties; they have to be understood as naming points on a curve of possibilities, as guesses or predictions rather than conclusions. Otherwise, scientists are in danger of reifying their concepts – of imputing an unvarying essence to phenomena that are in a continual state of flux. Peirce was the first scientist to perceive all the implications of this problem, and his philosophy . . . is obsessed with it. The problem boils down to this question: What does it mean to say that a statement "true" in a world is always susceptible to "a certain swerving"? (Menand 2001: 223)

This "swerving," this positive *reality* of chance is a basic element of the universe. Peirce called it "tychism" – based on the Greek word for chance. In one of his most speculative essays, "A Guess at the Riddle" (unpublished during his lifetime), he declares:

> We are brought, then, to this: conformity to law exists only within a limited range of events and even there is not perfect,

for an element of pure spontaneity or lawless originality mingles, or at least, must be supposed to mingle, with law everywhere. Moreover conformity with law is a fact requiring to be explained; and since Law in general cannot be explained by any law in particular, the explanation must consist in showing how law is developed out of pure chance, irregularity, and indeterminacy. ... According to this, three elements are active in the world: first chance; second law; and third habit-taking.

Such is our guess of the secret of the sphinx. (Peirce 1992: 276–7)

Peirce consistently argued that we can't understand the laws of nature unless we appreciate the positive role of chance – that it is a basic irreducible "element" active in a dynamic world. Typically, Peirce – in his speculations about the role of chance in the universe – was primarily concerned with clarifying the character of experimental science and the role of statistical probability in scientific explanation. James and Dewey sought to humanize Peirce's insight, and to bring out its rich ethical and political implications. The world in which we live is an "open universe" in which there is real chance, luck, and contingency. Contingency is a source of both joy and tragedy; it presents us with an opportunity and a challenge. Human agents can make a difference in shaping the world, although to do so intelligently requires sustained, rigorous inquiry. The reality of chance and contingency also means that we can never anticipate fully what will happen. This reinforces the necessity of developing critical flexible habits and practices that can help us cope with unexpected contingencies.

The pragmatists, Dewey in particular, are sometimes accused of being naïvely optimistic about what we can do and achieve. But when Dewey himself turned to what he called metaphysics, as the study of "the existential world in which we live," he told us that there is good reason to appeal to misfortunes and mistakes as evidence of the precarious nature of the world.

> Man finds himself living in an aleatory world; his existence involves, to put it baldly, a gamble. The world is a scene of risk; it is uncertain, unstable, uncannily unstable. Its dangers are irregular, inconstant, not to be counted upon as to their times and seasons. Plague, famine, failure of crops, disease, death, defeat in battle, are always just around the corner, and so are abundance, strength, victory, festival and song. Luck is proverbially both good and bad in its distribution. (Dewey 1981: 278)

We can never control our destinies completely or fully anticipate unexpected contingencies, but we can learn how to respond to them intelligently. Consequently, the mentality of pragmatic fallibilism is neither optimistic nor pessimistic; it is *practical* and *realistic*.

2

The Anticipations and Legacy of Pragmatic Fallibilism

In the epilogue to his book, Menand concludes his historical narrative by declaring "that a movement of thought that had grown out of the experience of the Civil War appeared to reach an end with the Cold War" (Menand 2001: 438). Before examining critically what he means by this, I want to return to a claim that I made in the previous chapter about mentalities. I suggested that mentalities take a variety of historical forms. Thus far I have explored the mentality of pragmatic fallibilism and its contrast with a mentality that appeals to absolutes, certainties, and stark oppositions of good and evil. The pragmatists never claimed to be completely original. On the contrary, when James spoke of "pragmatism," he characterized it as a new name for an old way of thinking. The pragmatic thinkers are rich and varied, because they drew upon different philosophical traditions in working out their ideas. Peirce initially drew his inspiration from Kant. He claimed to have studied the *Critique of Pure Reason* so thoroughly that he knew it virtually by heart. He appropriated the expression "pragmatic" from Kant's anthropological writings. As a young man, Dewey was inspired by Hegel – although Dewey's Hegel was a thinker who anticipated Dewey's own pragmatic experimentalism. Dewey "drifted away" from Hegel, and Darwin

replaced Hegel as his hero. But Dewey recognized that
Hegel's dynamic organic conception of experience left
a permanent deposit in his own thinking. James was
always drawn to the British empiricists, even though he
sharply criticized their tendency to think of experience as
an aggregate of bits of discrete, atomic impressions. In
his essay "What Pragmatism Means," he declared that
pragmatism is continuous with the empiricist attitude in
philosophy.

> Pragmatism represents a perfectly familiar attitude in phil-
> osophy, the empiricist attitude, but it represents it, as it
> seems to me, both in more radical and less objectionable
> form than it has ever yet assumed. A pragmatist turns his
> back resolutely and once and for all upon a lot of inveterate
> habits dear to professional philosophers. He turns away
> from abstraction and insufficiency, from verbal solutions,
> from bad *a priori* reasons, from fixed principles, closed
> systems, and pretended absolutes and origins. He turns
> towards concreteness and adequacy towards facts, towards
> action and towards power. That means the empiricist
> temper regnant and the rationalist temper sincerely given
> up. It means open air and possibilities of nature, as against
> dogma, artificiality, and the pretence of finality in truth.
> (James 1977: 379)

The pragmatists borrowed freely and appropriated what
they found intellectually congenial, while ignoring or
rejecting what they thought should be discarded. They
recognized themes and insights in previous philosophers
that anticipated what they emphasized. They also recognized themselves as belonging to, and furthering the development of, an American tradition. This was especially true
of James, Holmes, and Dewey. "Pragmatism belongs to a
disestablishment impulse in American culture – an impulse
that drew strength from the writings of Emerson, who

attacked institutions and conformity, and from the ascendancy, after the Civil War, of evolutionary theories, which drew attention to the contingency of all social forms" (Menand 2001: 89). Cornel West, in his own narrative of the development of pragmatism, begins with Emerson as the key figure who initiated many of the themes that the pragmatists developed (West 1989: ch. 1). Dewey deeply admired Emerson. He declared: "Emerson stands for restoring to the common man that which in the name of religion, philosophy, of art and morality, has been embezzled from the common store and appropriated to sectarian and class use" (Dewey 1981: 29). But Dewey reaches back further in American history and looks upon his own pragmatic defense of creative democracy as having its roots in Jefferson's vision of democracy. Jefferson was always one of Dewey's heroes, because Jefferson's conception of democracy is moral through and through: in its foundations, its methods, and its ends. Like Jefferson's notion of the wards as "small republics," Dewey felt that democracy requires a vital local community life – an active civil society – in which there is debate, deliberation, and dialogue. In *The Public and its Problems*, he wrote:

> Unless local communal life can be restored, the public cannot adequately solve its most urgent problem, to find and identify itself. But if it is reestablished, it will manifest a fullness, variety and freedom of possession and enjoyment of meanings and goods unknown in the contiguous associations of the past. For it will be alive and flexible as well as stable, responsive to the complex and worldwide scene in which it is enmeshed. While local, it will not be isolated. (Dewey 1927: 216)

I have been focusing on the historical situatedness of pragmatic fallibilism in the American context because I believe it represents what is best in this tradition. But this fallibilistic mentality stands in sharp conflict to another American tradition, which dates back to the Puritans – one that is drawn to absolutes, moral certainties, and sharp dichotomies of good and evil. At different stages in our history, the conflict of mentalities has broken out with renewed vigor. And today, in a post-9/11 world – a world in which there are all sorts of new unanticipated dangers – we are once again engaged in a fierce battle of clashing mentalities. But there is nothing *uniquely* American about pragmatic fallibilism; it has a more universal and global reach. The pragmatists were "rooted cosmopolitans." They were *rooted* in, and responsive to, the conflicts in American life, but they were *cosmopolitan* in their aspirations and vision.

In the first lecture of *A Pluralistic Universe*, James makes an extremely perceptive remark. He tells us:

> If we take the whole history of philosophy, the systems reduce themselves to a few main types which, under all the technical verbiage in which the ingenious intellect of man envelopes them, are just so many visions, modes of feeling the whole push, and seeing the whole drift of life, forced on one by one's total character and experience, and on the whole preferred – there is no other truthful word – as one's best working attitude. (James 1977: 489)

This dovetails with what James writes about the role of temperament in philosophy.

> The history of philosophy is to a great extent that of a certain clash of human temperaments. Undignified as such a treatment may seem to some of my colleagues, I shall have to take account of this clash and explain a good many of the divergences of philosophers by it. Of whatever temperament a professional philosopher is, he tries, when philosophizing, to sink the fact of his temperament. Temperament is no

conventionally recognized reason, so he urges impersonal reasons only for his conclusions. Yet temperament really gives him a stronger bias than any of his more strictly object-ive premises. (James 1977: 363)

Some philosophers have been scandalized by these claims. They accuse James of a rampant "subjectivism" – a denial of the neutrality and objectivity that philosophy ought to strive to achieve. But I believe that James is being brutally honest and extremely insightful. What James means by "vision" and "temperament" is close to what I am calling "mentality." James certainly does *not* denigrate the role of argument in philosophy. It is all important. Vision without argument becomes sentimental, and argu-ments without vision are pedantic and sterile. When James speaks of these visions being forced on one by one's total character and *experience*, he is certainly recognizing that they are not "merely" subjective or arbitrary. But if we approach different philosophers in this manner, with focus on their "visions, modes of feeling the whole push, and seeing the whole drift of life," then we can see how the men-tality embodied in pragmatic fallibilism has a much broader, deeper, and universal significance. Philosophers working in very different traditions and historical contexts share a similar vision and exhibit a similar temperament in their approach to thinking, action, and feeling.

I want to illustrate this by considering briefly two influ-ential contemporary philosophers whose work is congenial to pragmatic fallibilism: Charles Taylor and Jürgen Habermas. I am *not* claiming that Taylor and Habermas are pragmatists. Some of their differences from the pragmatic thinkers are as striking as anything that they have in common with them. And the differences between Taylor and Habermas are also consequential. In philosophy and social theory, it is frequently the differences that make all the difference in the world. But I am suggesting that if we take the kind of approach suggested by James, we can recognize how close they are to the pragmatic thinkers – how they exhibit the same mentality – the same philosophical temperament and vision.

We can see this by turning again to the theses that Putnam enumerated as constitutive of the pragmatic "way of thinking": anti-skepticism, fallibilism, the denial of a dichotomy of fact and value, and the primacy of practice. Taylor and Habermas would endorse all of these theses. They have elaborated them in ways that enrich pragmatic fallibilism. Thus, for example, Charles Taylor has been one of the sharpest critics of a positivist conception of the social sciences based on the rigid dichotomy of fact and value. And Habermas, from his own early comments on the "positivist debate" through his theory of cognitive interests to the elaboration of his theory of communicative action, has challenged the fact–value dichotomy and the separation of facts and norms. Both Taylor and Habermas have consistently affirmed fallibilism. Taylor draws on the phenomenological and hermeneutical tradition to develop his version of fallibilism and the openness of dialogue. And Habermas has been a relentless critic of total systems that claim completeness and necessity. His idea of "postmetaphysical thinking" is a version of fallibilism that must be responsive to ongoing public criticism. Both Taylor and Habermas have a vital sense of a world of unexpected contingencies. This shapes their understanding of the relation of theory and practice. Both are sharp critics of all forms of dogmatism and ideologies, and both have criticized some of the excesses of a "postmodernism" that denies objective validity and celebrates relativism. They have sought to defend the role of open dialogical communication as fundamental to a democratic deliberation. The issue of cultural pluralism has been central for both of them. What is fascinating about their own debates concerning multiculturalism is the way they echo the tensions that were prominent in the pragmatic debates in the 1920s. Taylor is closer to Horace Kallen's understanding of cultural pluralism, with its emphasis on the need to protect the rights of different groups in order to secure their continued existence. And Habermas is closer to Dewey, who worries about the dangers of reifying cultural separatism.[1]

But there is another dimension of their understanding of the relation of theory and practice that brings them even closer to the pragmatists – especially John Dewey. Both have been public intellectuals very much in the spirit of Dewey. Taylor is the leading Canadian public philosopher of his generation, just as Habermas is the leading German public intellectual. Like Dewey, they have not only contributed to professional philosophical concerns, but have consistently addressed the critical political and social issues of their time in the public media. As with Dewey, their theoretical concerns grow out of their awareness of concrete social and political conflicts. At the core of their vision stands the project of rethinking what democracy means in a complex technological global world – a world in which there are powerful forces distorting and undermining the flourishing of democracy. Taylor and Habermas, like Dewey before them, have sought to identify and probe the most serious threats and dangers that democracy faces in a global world dominated by instrumental and technological thinking.

Taylor, a native of Montreal, grew up in a bilingual and bicultural home, with an English-speaking Protestant father and a French-speaking Catholic mother. He has always been concerned with the problem of political fragmentation and the eclipse of public life. For more than 40 years, he has sought to elaborate an understanding and

ideal of "deep diversity" that is at once sensitive to the
recognition of different cultural identities yet strives to
achieve a genuine commonality. And if one wants to understand Habermas's philosophical project and the vision that
stands at the heart of his thinking, then one must relate it
to the central intellectual and emotional crisis of his life. It
was his discovery just after the Second World War – when
he was still in his teens – of the full scope of the horrors of
the Nazi period. All of Habermas's thinking can be related
to his lifelong attempt not simply to understand what
happened to Germany at that dark time, but to articulate
and defend a deliberative democratic alternative. Both
Taylor and Habermas have also been cosmopolitan
thinkers. They draw upon different philosophical traditions in developing their own philosophical visions of a
global democracy that is sensitive to cultural and national
differences. In philosophical terms, they seek to combine a
respect for difference and otherness within a context of
concrete universality. It is not surprising that Habermas's
vision is so close to pragmatic fallibilism, because Peirce,
Dewey, and Mead have deeply influenced his philosophical
investigations. Habermas has always recognized how close
his temperament and outlook are to those of the pragmatic
thinkers. And recently, Charles Taylor has come to recognize his intellectual affinities with William James.[2]

I want to reiterate what I stated earlier. My intention is
not to show that Taylor and Habermas are "really" pragmatists. Rather, I want to show how the mentality that
informs their work exhibits a profound affinity with pragmatic fallibilism. Both Taylor and Habermas share
Dewey's democratic faith "in the role of consultation, of
conference, of persuasion, in the formation of public
opinion which is in the long run self-corrective" (Dewey
1939: 227). This basic conviction animates the thinking of
Dewey, Habermas, and Taylor.

If we consider once again what William James says about temperament and vision in determining one's way of thinking and acting, then we can see how close Habermas and Taylor are to the pragmatic thinkers. They exhibit and share the mentality of pragmatic fallibilism. And this commonality exemplifies my basic claim that the same mentality informs philosophical projects that arise in different historical settings.

I want to return to Menand's narrative of the fate of the pragmatic thinkers in the United States. Although his remarks are sketchy, Menand suggests that it was the Cold War that was primarily responsible for their demise.

> Holmes, James, Peirce, and Dewey wished to bring ideas and principles and beliefs down to a human level because they wished to avoid the violence they saw hidden in abstractions. This is one of the lessons the Civil War had taught them. The political system their philosophy was designed to support was democracy. And democracy, as they understood it, isn't just letting the right people have their say: it's also about letting the wrong people have their say. It is about giving space to minority and dissenting views so that, at the end of the day, the interests of the majority may prevail. (Menand 2001: 440)

But the Cold War represented a very different style of thinking and mentality, one that displaced the open, experimental, fallibilistic attitude of the pragmatic thinkers.

> The Cold War was a war over principles.. . . A style of thought that elevated compromise over confrontation therefore did not hold much appeal. Even the opponents of the Cold War mounted their opposition on principle. The notion that values of the free society, for which the Cold War was waged were contingent, relative, fallible constructions, good for some purposes and not good for others, was not a

notion compatible with the moral imperatives of the age.
(Menand 2001: 441)

And in a final coda, Menand tells us:

> And once the Cold War ended, the ideas of Holmes, James
> Peirce and Dewey emerged as suddenly as they had been
> eclipsed. The writers began to be studied and debated with
> a seriousness and intensity, both in the United States and in
> other countries, that they had not attracted for forty years,
> For in the post-Cold War world, where there are many
> competing belief systems, not just two, skepticism about the
> finality of any particular set of beliefs has begun to seem to
> some people an important value again. And so has the polit-
> ical theory this skepticism helps to underwrite: the theory of
> democracy is the value that validates all other values.
> Democratic participation isn't the means to an end, in this
> way of thinking; it is the end. The purpose of the experiment
> is to keep the experiment going. (Menand 2001: 441)

Menand wrote these words shortly before 9/11 – and
since that infamous date, there has been a radical shift in
the dominant ways of thinking. One must not underestimate the consequential differences of the American Civil
War, the Cold War, and the new "War on Terror." Each of
these occurred in radically different historical circumstances, with very different origins and causes. Yet there are
some disturbing similarities in the mentality that gained
dominance in these different times and circumstances.
There is an appeal to rigid principles, moral certainties,
and confrontation. There are no nuances here, but only the
white-and-black opposition of good and evil. This is a
quasi-Manichaean world. It is *quasi*-Manichaean, because
the original Manichaeans believed that God is *coeternal*
with Satan. Consequently there can be no final victory
over evil. But today we are told that ultimately Good will

triumph over Evil. We hear this not only from our own political leaders, but also from those militant Islamic fanatics who are convinced of the righteousness of their cause. Both sides are convinced that God is on their side, and will vindicate their cause. Any deviation from this stark opposition is interpreted as a sign of vacillation and weakness. And there is also a pernicious sexual subtext here. The "masculine" virtues of toughness, strength, decisiveness, determination to stay the course, are accentuated. Those who oppose this are "feminized." They are sensitive, indecisive, and weak. They are "girlie-men."

It is true that the absolute low point – the nadir – of the influence of pragmatism in America coincided with the origins of the Cold War, and that a great revival of interest in pragmatism has taken place since the passing of the Cold War. But the full story of the demise and resurgence of pragmatism is – as Menand himself notes – more complicated. Many factors contributed to the marginalization of the pragmatic thinkers. During the decades preceding the Second World War, there was a rapid growth of professionalism in academic philosophy departments. There was a new emphasis on technical, logical, and argumentative finesse among philosophers, with little concern for broader political and social issues. At the height of his popularity, Dewey called passionately for philosophers to enlarge their vision, to turn away from an exclusive concern with the traditional problems of philosophy and to focus their attention on the "problems of men" – the problems that human beings face in their everyday lives. But by the 1950s, many academic philosophers were obsessively concerned with the "problems of philosophy" – and with *dissolving* them. The very idea of the philosopher as a public intellectual who would address the "problems of men" was ridiculed. The discipline of philosophy became so specialized and so esoteric that few persons outside the discipline saw that it had much relevance. During the past few decades, however, there has been a resurgence of pragmatism.[3] But this interest is still been primarily limited to academic circles. There is no intellectual figure in America today who has the influence and appeal of thinkers like Holmes, James, or Dewey.[4]

But there is another way to understand the vicissitudes of a fallibilistic pragmatic orientation. As a historical philosophical movement, there is much in the classical pragmatic thinkers that is dated and irrelevant for us today. This makes perfect sense from a pragmatic point of view. As strong advocates of ongoing self-corrective inquiry, the pragmatic thinkers would be the first to claim that this also applies to the claims advanced by the pragmatists themselves. With their consciousness that philosophical speculation is always grounded in its concrete historical context, they would also insist philosophy must be rethought in light of the new problems and conflicts that emerge in different historical contexts. *But there is a vital core of the pragmatic ethos that is enduring and transcends the historical context in which it emerged.* Peirce, James, and Dewey did think – for the most part – that once the quest for certainty was exposed, once the craving for absolutes was challenged, once we learned that there is no permanent metaphysical comfort and that we must cope intelligently with unexpected contingencies and dangers, then there would be no going back – no return to a world of simple binary oppositions of Good and Evil. *But they were wrong.* They underestimated the appeal of the mentality they opposed – especially in times of perceived crisis, anxiety, and fear. But with the hope that a pragmatic fallible mentality would prevail, there was always the realization that it requires constant and persistent effort to make the virtues and practices of a fallibilistic mentality a living reality. It is not easy to live with contingency and uncertainty. There is a deep craving for security and certainty – and there is always the possibility of a *regression* to a more simplified world of black-and-white dichotomies – a simplified world in which there is no ambiguity about Good and Evil. To institute a fallibilistic ethos as living reality in people's everyday lives requires passionate commitment and persistence, because this ethos is always under threat. And today the threats are more serious and more ominous than they have ever been. We are told that we are engaged in a new kind of war that is different from all other wars – a "War on Terror." And to win this war, we do not have the luxury of being pragmatic fallibilists.

What we are confronting today – since 9/11 – is a clash of mentalities. And this is a clash that cuts across morality, politics, and religion. It manifests itself in *all* areas of human experience. It is fashionable today to associate the quest for certainty and the craving for absolutes with religion. When the president of the most powerful nation in the world appeals to the Almighty to justify controversial political and military decisions, and sees himself as the leader of the battle against Evil, when he adopts an apocalyptic rhetoric, it is not difficult to understand why his critics are so skeptical of these "religious" claims. And without underestimating the crucial differences, it is alarming to see parallels with those militants who appeal to God to justify a jihad – a holy war – against the evil infidels. But the problem is *not* religion. Rather, it is the mentality that prevails in religion. Within the great world religions, we find the same clash of mentalities. The mentality of pragmatic fallibilism is *not* anti-religious; it is anti-dogmatic and anti-ideological.

The point that I want to emphasize goes beyond pragmatism. In the great religious traditions there have always been believers who have argued that a genuine religious faith is one that is open to questioning. We must not confuse religious faith with ideological fanaticism. And we must passionately oppose ideological fanaticism wherever it arises – regardless of whether it takes a religious or a non-religious form. We must passionately oppose the abuse of evil wherein we demonize the enemy, oversimplify a complex reality by imposing facile dichotomies, make specious claims of certainty, and denigrate critical thinking.

3

Moral Certainty and Passionate Commitment

In the previous chapters I described the mentality of pragmatic fallibility and contrasted it with the appeal to
absolutes, moral certainties, and a black-and-white world
of good and evil. But the objection might well be raised
that I have ignored some tough issues. A critic might
object that I am guilty of presenting a new misleading
Either/Or: either pragmatic fallibility or the appeal to
absolutes. But such an Either/Or masks the real situation
that we confront today. Fallibilism may well be the preferred ethos in those situations in which we can expect
deliberation – where we are dealing with reasonable
persons who are open and willing to engage in critical dialogue. But this is not our situation today. It is a world in
which terrorism, which has become increasingly sophisti-
cated, poses radically new threats. We have to face the
realistic possibility that terrorists may soon have the chemical, biological, and even nuclear weapons to carry out
mass murder. It may well be that there is no single essence
or definition of what we take to be evil, but the deliberate
murder of innocent victims has always been an exemplar
of evil. The critic might point out that I have already
conceded that new forms of evil have burst forth in the
twentieth century. Why not recognize that we are now
facing a new form of evil? The trouble with the pragmatists

is that they have always felt uncomfortable with facing up to evil. "Evil" is not really a part of their vocabulary. They speak of contingencies and dangers, but they are unrealistic about the *real* dangers that now exist. Deliberation, diplomacy, and persuasion are, of course, desirable. But we have to realize that – to use a pragmatic turn of phrase – they do not work in the extreme circumstances that exist today in the "War on Terror." We are dealing with ruthless fanatical murderers. We have to be decisive, forceful, steadfast, and fully committed to fighting this new evil. The real weakness with pragmatism is that it lacks the resources to justify decisiveness and passionate commitment. Such a commitment depends on a firm conviction – the moral and political certainty that one's cause is just. Otherwise we will lack the will and persistence to make the sacrifices required for fighting the enemy. The primary issue is the eminently *practical* one of doing what is required to fight this new evil. Pragmatists are always telling us that we should judge ideas by their consequences. Despite the well-intentioned claims of the pragmatists, the real consequences of this mentality are indecisiveness and a fluctuating equivocation that undermines principled commitment and clear decisive action.

The objection is a serious one, and it needs to be confronted squarely. It is a variation of the familiar charge that pragmatism is naïvely optimistic and does not fully appreciate the tragic dark side of human life, the sinfulness of human beings, and the intransigence of evil. During Dewey's lifetime, Reinhold Niebuhr pressed this criticism against him. More recently, it has been reiterated by Jack Diggins. Even Cornel West, who thinks of himself as working in the pragmatic tradition, worries about whether pragmatists really have the resources to deal with evil.[1]

Sidney Hook has given one of the sharpest and best responses to the caricature of pragmatism as being naïvely optimistic and lacking the resources to deal with tragedy and evil. Hook was a student and a close associate of John Dewey. As a young man, before his pragmatic turn, he identified himself with a Hegelian–Marxist tradition, but he became one of the most penetrating and forceful critics of communism at a time when many American liberals were still fellow travelers. He was known as the "bulldog" of the pragmatists. His 1974 book, *Pragmatism and the Tragic Sense of Life*, provides a strong critical response to the recurring objection that pragmatism is superficial and naïve. The essays collected in that volume exhibit a vitality and a freshness that make them highly relevant to our contemporary situation.[2] Hook succinctly summarizes the familiar caricature of pragmatism "as a superficial philosophy of optimism, of uncritical adjustment and conformity, of worship of the goddess of success." This distortion, based on a tendentious reading of Peirce, James, and Dewey, misses what is most central to the pragmatic temper.

> Pragmatism was not only a method of clarifying ideas by exploring their consequences in behavioral use. It was also a temper of mind towards the vital options which men confront when they become aware of what alternative proposals commit them to. It stressed the efficacy of ideals and actions and at the same time their inescapable limitations. It foreswore the promise of total solutions and wholesale salvation for piecemeal gains. Yet far from embracing easy formulae of the ultimate reconciliation of conflicting interests and values, it acknowledged the reality of piecemeal losses even when we risk our lives to achieve the gains. (Hook 1974: 4–5)

We are frequently faced with hard choices and conflicting options where there is *no* possibility – even after careful deliberation – of reconciling "conflicting interests and values." And in making these choices we need to be acutely aware of our limitations.

> No matter how intelligent and humane our choices, there are, as William James insists, "real losses and real losers." We live in a dangerous and adventurous and serious world and "the very 'seriousness'," James goes on to say, "we attribute to life means that the ineluctable noes and losses form part of it, that there are genuine sacrifices, and that something permanently drastic and bitter always remains at the bottom of the cup." (Hook 1974: 5)

This is the aspect of pragmatism that has been ignored by its critics, but it is stands at the heart of pragmatism. Pragmatism, Hook claims, is grounded in a recognition of "the tragic sense of life," an expression that he appropriated from the Spanish philosopher Miguel de Unamuno. What, precisely, does Hook mean by the tragic sense of life?

> Every genuine experience of moral doubt and perplexity in which we ask "What should I do?" takes place in a situation where good conflicts with good. If we already know what is evil, the moral inquiry is over, or it never really begins. "The worse or evil," Dewey says, "is the rejected good," but until we reject it, the situation is one in which apparent good opposes apparent good. "All the serious perplexities of life come back to the genuine difficulty of forming a judgment as to the values of a situation; they come back to a conflict of goods." No matter how we resolve the situation, some good will be sacrificed, some interest, whose immediate craving for satisfaction may be every whit as intense and authentic as its fellows, will be modified, frustrated or even suppressed. (Hook 1974: 13)

There are "small tragedies" in life, but the tragic quality of moral dilemmas emerges most dramatically when the conflicts and choices we face are – to use William James's expressions – *momentous* and *forced*. As Dewey tells us, "only the conventional and the fanatical are always immediately sure of right and wrong [or good and evil] in conduct."

We not only have to make difficult choices, but, as Hook emphasizes, we are frequently faced with moral and political dilemmas where there are incompatible and irreconcilable values. This is precisely why pragmatists place so much emphasis on deliberation, inquiry, and the careful evaluation of consequences of our decisions and actions. The pragmatists do not underestimate the role of conflict in human life – even irreconcilable conflicts. Dewey makes the perceptive observation that if we already know what is evil, then moral inquiry is over, or it never really begins. Simply *labeling* something or some person as evil is *not* moral inquiry. For all the emotional appeal of this labeling, it obscures and distorts our choices. The pragmatists stress the *agent's perspective* – the perspective of those who have to make choices and decisions. The primary question is always how to *respond* to what we take to be dangerous, threatening, or unjust situations. And when we conclude that someone or something is evil, we should be prepared to explain and justify what we mean, because we still have to decide how we will respond to this concrete evil. In making moral or political choices there is always the need for deliberation and questioning, and there is also always the possibility of disagreement. Reasonable persons can and do disagree about what is to be done. Furthermore, we frequently have to act without the opportunity to engage in full deliberative inquiry. This is why the pragmatists stress the need to cultivate those habits, dispositions, and practices that will enable us to act decisively. It is a misleading caricature of the pragmatic mentality to suggest that it calls for endless debate. It is difficult to think of another philosophical orientation that has placed so much emphasis on conduct, practice, and action. There is no incompatibility between being *decisive* and recognizing the *fallibility* and limitations of our choices and decisions. On the contrary, this is what is required for *responsible* action. We must recognize that whatever we do, there will always be unintended and unpredictable consequences. Acknowledging and intelligently assessing these consequences may require altering our conduct. Fallibilism takes seriously the commonsense realization that we learn – or *ought* to learn – from our mistakes. And because of human finitude and limitation, we cannot avoid making mistakes. It takes imagination and courage to acknowledge our mistakes. "Steadfastness" and "staying the course" are not virtues but *vices* when they involve ignoring the undesirable consequences of our choices and actions. "Aside . . . from the cruelty of those who glory in the personal harm they can inflict, the possibility of cruelty is the ever-present converse fact of human limitation. We are all crueler than we know, not because we are evil, but because our senses and imagination have such a limited range" (Hook 1974: 29).

One must not confuse flexibility and reflective intelligence with indecisiveness. The appeal to evil is being used today to "justify" deeply problematic and questionable courses of action. In the abuse of evil there is a manipulative – and sometimes cynical – *fusing* together of widely disparate phenomena into a single, reified evil enemy. Saddam Hussein, Osama bin Laden, Palestinian suicide bombers, and Chechnyan rebels are lumped together as if they were a single evil enemy – or part of a single global conspiracy.[3] And the *factual evidence* making it clear that this is just not so – and that it is politically disastrous to think that there is a single "evil force" threatening our security – is ignored or deliberately suppressed. The very expression "War on Terror" is deeply misleading. Terror is not an enemy; terror is a complex of tactics and strategies used by different groups for different purposes. But those who are all too eager to label the enemy as evil or as part of the "Axis of Evil" are impatient with this obvious fact. The abuse of evil – the reification of evil – also blocks serious inquiry into why so many people throughout the world sympathize with terrorists. It blocks inquiry into a phenomenon that is taking on global significance – the rage expressed by those who believe that they are constantly and systematically being *humiliated*. Humiliation is one of the primary social and political forces in this global world – and there is still little real understanding of its power to motivate people. There are not only the evils of fanatical terrorists, but also the evils of those whose actions inflict humiliation. There are "great ranges of cruelty in modern history, involving the fate of millions, that flow from the limitations of human imagination and sensitivity, of cruelty men do because it is easy to stand what is out of sight, and still easier to stand what is out of mind" (Hook 1974: 29). There is also a failure to raise questions about whether the tactics and strategies employed in combating our "evil enemies" may have the unintended consequence of creating an environment in which terrorists will continue to flourish. Like Proteus, terrorism takes on ever new forms. And if we are honest, there is good reason to believe that we can never *completely* eliminate terrorist initiatives. What we can do is try to eliminate known terrorists, and, as Samantha Power reminds us, "undertake the complex and elaborate effort to distinguish sympathizers from militants and keep its converts to a minimum. Terrorism also requires understanding how our past policies helped to give to such venomous grievances" (2004: 37). But today those who seek to raise and debate such issues are frequently accused of being unpatriotic.

"Realization of the evil men can do and have done to men is integral to any intelligent appraisal of human history" (Hook 1974: 30). We must recognize the variety of sources of concrete evils. They can flow from "ignorance, insensitiveness and imaginative dullness of even conventionally good men." The post-9/11 discourse about evil is *regressive* because it is based on one of the most *primitive* conceptions of evil. We demonize the enemy, think of the enemy as possessed by Satan – as someone who does evil for evil's sake. But the lesson that we should have learned from the twentieth century, from the writings of Hannah Arendt, Primo Levi, and many others is that the worst evils we experience cannot be adequately understood if we think of them as exclusively the actions of vicious demonized individuals.

> There is intelligent and unintelligent fear ... Intelligent fear arms us against real dangers and enables us, by modifying the environment or altering our behavior, to reduce the incidence of terror and pain. Intelligent fear must be proportionate to the dangers. It is the absence of any proportion between the danger and the fear which marks the panicky and hysterical response. Political thinking is often distorted by a failure to distinguish between fears that are ill-grounded or well-grounded. (Hook 1974: 58)

"The grim fact, however, is that there is sometimes no desire to reason, no wish to negotiate except as a holding action to accumulate strategic power, nothing but the reliance of one party or the other upon brute force even when other alternatives may exist" (Hook 1974: 23). The pragmatist mentality recognizes that there are *limits* to tolerance. We cannot tolerate those who are *actively* intolerant – those who seek to undermine the very possibility of discourse, dialogue, and rational persuasion. But how are we to decide when these limits have been reached? What is the criterion for deciding when there is a legitimate use of force? From a pragmatic perspective, these questions cannot be answered in an *abstract* manner. They demand specificity, inquiry into the historical circumstances, and risky choices. But if the virtues and practices of robust pragmatic fallibilism prevail, there will be a willingness to listen to dissenting voices and an openness to modifying our conduct in light of the intelligent evaluation of the consequences of our choices and actions. There will also be a strong resistance to the curtailment of civil liberties.

Still, it may be objected that however noble the pragmatic appeal to discussion, dialogue, and persuasion, it fails to grasp the character of fanaticism that is motivated by irrational passions. This is also an objection that Reinhold Niebuhr pressed against John Dewey. Niebuhr accused Dewey of being a rationalist who rested his hopes on self-sufficient reason. But Dewey rightly responded that this was a caricature of the pragmatic conception of social intelligence. Dewey preferred to speak of intelligence rather than reason because he objected to the way in which many traditional philosophers had characterized reason – as if it were a special faculty that had intrinsic power. Intelligence is not an autonomous faculty, but consists of a set of habits, dispositions, and virtues that are not innate but need to be cultivated. In response to Niebuhr, Dewey affirmed that "intelligence has no power per se." It becomes powerful "only as it is integrated into some system of wants, of effective demands." Pragmatism does not deny the strength of human emotions and passions. The point is to *inform* these passions with intelligence, to make them more humane.

The critics of a pragmatic temper frequently present themselves as "tough-minded realists," who mock their opponents as "tender-minded sentimentalists."[4] But Hook gives a piercing rejoinder to this charge. What he wrote in 1947 might well have been written in 2005.

This "tough-mindedness" is another expression of the abdication of intelligence. It refuses to discuss the specific problems and the specific ways of handling them, smothering all problems under a blanket allegiance to some vaguely defined goal. It wraps itself up in the blind faith, essentially religious, that no matter what is done, things will come right in the end. It is impatient with any attempt to judge verbal professions by consequences in fact. It is really not an attitude of tough-mindedness at all, for it cannot face or live with the truth. It cannot bear to see its assumptions put into the crucible of doubt. Rather it is a tender-minded sentimentalism that reads its pious wishes into the mysterious "workings" of history. (Hook 1974: 35)

We come here to the heart of the matter – to what is implicitly presupposed in the objection that I rehearsed at the beginning of this chapter. It is the unspoken assumption that "tough-minded realism," strength, forcefulness, decisiveness, and persistence are based upon unwavering *moral certainty*. For without a firm, absolute, moral conviction, we will lack the determination to do what is required to fight evil. But here is where we detect the gross fallacious slide from *subjective moral certitude* to alleged *objective moral certainty*. The strength of one's personal conviction is *never sufficient* to justify the truth or correctness of one's claims. This is the primary lesson of pragmatic fallibilism. Furthermore, we need to expose the vulgar form of the Cartesian Anxiety that corrupts so much of current political rhetoric. We are presented with the alternatives of *either* steadfast moral certainty *or* a wishy-washy vacillating relativism. And the not-so-hidden implication is that pragmatic fallibility is effeminate and tender-minded; it lacks the guts to cope with the evil of terror. Over and over again, so-called tough-minded realists affirm this in conscious and subliminal ways. We need to bring this attitude out into the open and expose it. It is based on confusion between subjective *certitude* and objective *certainty*. Ideologists, fanatics, and fundamentalists are always claiming certainty. History is full of instances of discarded certainties. As Peirce noted long ago, we are confronted with conflicting, contradictory claims about certainty. The fervor with which one asserts the possession of moral certainties is *no evidence whatsoever* for the truth or validity of one's claims. One of the original motivations for the development of pragmatism was the realization that tenacious professions of certitude are *never* sufficient to justify the truth of our beliefs. Peirce called this the method of tenacity for fixing belief. And what he wrote in 1877 is still – perhaps even more – relevant for us today.

> The instinctive dislike of an undecided state of mind, exaggerated into a vague dread of doubt, makes men cling spasmodically to the views they already take. The man feels that, if he only holds his belief without wavering, it will be entirely satisfactory. Nor can it be denied that a steady and immovable faith yields great peace of mind . . . And in many cases it may well be that the pleasure he derives from his calm faith overbalances any inconveniences resulting from its deceptive character. (Peirce 1992: 116)

Earlier I mentioned the rather innocuous situation in which I declare that I am *absolutely certain* that I saw someone only to discover that I was mistaken. But there are horrendous situations where professions of absolute certainty are extremely dangerous and systematically misleading – if not deceitful. In justifying the "preventive war," the US administration bombarded us with their absolutely certain knowledge that Saddam Hussein possessed weapons of mass destruction.[5]

> The supposition that the Bush people truly believed in their WMD nightmare was indicated by the unconditional

quality of their prose. Phrases like "we do know, with absolute certainty," uttered with majestic authority, abounded in Vice President Cheney's speeches. He was also a "no doubt" man in, "There is no doubt that Saddam Hussein now has weapons of mass destruction." The president was another "no doubt" man: "Intelligence gathered by this and other governments leaves no doubt that the Iraq regime continues to possess and conceal some of the most lethal weapons ever devised." Asked about the location of the WMDs, Secretary of Defense Rumsfeld said confidently: "We know where they are." (Schlesinger 2004: 29)

But we now know that all these "no doubt" statements and "absolute certainty" claims were *false*. Moreover, we also know that doubts about the reliability of this intelligence information were systematically discounted. There has been extensive discussion of whether Bush and his administration genuinely and sincerely believed what they claimed to know with absolute certainty or whether they were deliberately lying. Defenders of the administration claim that our leaders genuinely believed that there were weapons of mass destruction and that Saddam Hussein *did* pose on "imminent threat." But the question must be asked: why were our leaders so ready and eager to believe that Hussein possessed these weapons? One cannot underestimate the power of the *mentality* that gripped the administration – especially the president's tendency to see the world in the stark terms of good and evil. Greg Thielmann, a member of the State Department's Bureau of Intelligence and Research, claims that the Bush administration had a "faith-based intelligence attitude: 'We know the answers, give us the intelligence to support these answers.'" Peter Singer adds:

> It seems probable that it was not faith in general that gave Bush and his aides a misplaced confidence that they knew the answers. It was the idea that Saddam was evil.

Writing in *Newsweek* on how Bush justified going to war with Iraq, Howard Fineman observed, "He decided that Saddam was evil, and everything follows from that." That alone made it intuitively obvious that Saddam must be building weapons of mass destruction. But it is a mistake to divide the world neatly into good and evil, black and white without shades of gray, in a manner that eliminates the need to learn more about those with whom one is dealing. For an unreflective person, having a sense of "moral clarity" that disregards the shadings in human motivation and conduct can be a vice, not a virtue. (Singer 2004: 211–12)

But why is the appeal to certainty so seductive when it comes to issues of choice, decision, and action? It is because of the belief that unless we do possess this certainty, we will not have any basis for justifying our choices, decisions, and actions. *This is the faulty inference that must be exposed and rejected.* When we are acting intelligently, we appeal to reasons to justify our actions – or we should be prepared to do so if challenged. But when we appeal to reasons, we are operating in a space where there can be better and worse arguments based upon concrete evidence. If we give reasons to justify our actions, then we must admit that however plausible and convincing we find these arguments, they are *always* open to further inquiry and critique. There is no escape from fallibility. But does acknowledging the fallibility of our reasons and justifications mean that we will lack the conviction and passionate commitment to choose and act decisively? The answer is clearly No! We should act on what we take to be our best reasons and strongest convictions. We should be prepared to die for what we ultimately cherish. None of this requires any compromise or weakening of fallibilism – the belief that no matter how firmly we hold some fundamental beliefs, they are in principle open to criticism and self-correction. To use a different idiom, to acknowledge our fallibility is to recognize our *human finitude*. In his famous essay "Two Concepts of Liberty," Isaiah Berlin quotes a wise saying by Joseph Schumpeter, who wrote: "To realise the relative validity of one's convictions and yet stand for them unflinchingly, is what distinguishes a civilized man from a barbarian." And Berlin comments: "To demand more than this is perhaps a deep incurable metaphysical need; but to allow it to determine one's practice is a symptom of an equally deep, and more dangerous, moral and political immaturity" (Berlin 1969: 172).[6]

There is a residual belief that, ideally, it would be most desirable to achieve the type of indubitable certainty that could provide the foundation for our epistemological and moral judgments; but, as fallible human beings, we can never achieve such certainty. We have to settle for what is second best – fallible knowledge. But this really misses the central point of the pragmatists' insight. They are making a much stronger and more important claim. The very idea of epistemological or moral certainty is *incoherent*. In everyday life, we are *practically* certain about all sorts of things – even though we may discover that we are mistaken in our beliefs. But if we mean by "certainty" something that is incorrigible – something that can never be questioned, modified, or corrected, then the pragmatists are telling us that there is no such thing! That is why we have good reason to be skeptical with regard to anyone who tells us that they are *absolutely certain* that they know what is truly evil. Once we give up the specious idea of absolute moral certainty, then we have to think of our convictions and commitments in a different way. They ought to be based on our best and strongest reasons for acting. And the most effective way of testing these is by opening them to public discussion, debate, and criticism.

In short, we need to be critical of those who claim to know with absolute certainty what is good and evil, and who think that such moral certainty is the basis for decisiveness and passionate commitment to fight injustices and concrete evils. Our commitments and convictions will be stronger if they are informed by intelligent deliberation and tested by public discussion. Contrary to those who think that unless we achieve objective moral certainty, we will lack decisiveness and firm commitment to fight for what we believe is right and just, the reverse is true. Our passionate commitment to just causes is strengthened and deepened when we are prepared to justify them by an appeal to reasons and evidence that are subject to open, public, critical discussion. This is essential for a democracy that truly cherishes freedom.

4

Evil and the Corruption of Democratic Politics

In my introduction, I claimed that the post-9/11 discourse of good and evil is *anti-political* and *anti-religious*. This might seem to be counter-intuitive and perplexing. After all, whether we like it or not, there are frequent references to evil in the speeches of politicians, especially in the United States.[1] And it certainly appears to be extremely politically effective – in arousing deep emotions and political support. Furthermore, Bush and those in sympathy with him, are constantly "justifying" their discourse of good and evil by an appeal to their religious convictions and faith in the Almighty. So, it may well be asked, what does it mean to say that this new appeal to good and evil is anti-religious? I want to argue that when we probe the meaning of both democratic politics and religious faith, we see how the new discourse of good and evil corrupts both politics and religion. In this chapter I will focus on democratic politics, and in the following chapter on religion and faith.

In exploring the meaning of politics, I begin by drawing on the insights of Hannah Arendt. Arendt is now recognized as one of the most perceptive and challenging political theorists of the twentieth century, and I believe that many of her insights must be incorporated in any fully adequate conception of democratic politics.[2] She once claimed that all thinking "arises out of the actuality of incidents, and incidents of living experience must remain guideposts by which it takes its bearings if it is not to lose itself in the heights to which thinking soars, or in the depths to which it must descend." The horrendous experience that profoundly shaped her thinking was her encounter with totalitarianism, especially Nazi totalitarianism. In an interview in 1964, Arendt was asked: "Is there a definite event in your memory that dates your turn to the political?" Without hesitating, she answered: "I would say February 27, 1933, the burning of the *Reichstag*, and the illegal arrests that followed during the same night." From that moment on, she "felt responsible." "That is, I was no longer of the opinion that one can simply be a bystander" (Arendt 1994: 4). In the following months, Arendt helped others to escape from Nazi Germany. She also aided her Zionist friends. This activity led to the incident that forced her to flee Germany. She was asked by her German Zionist friends to help document Nazi anti-Semitic propaganda. Despite the danger, she readily agreed to help. Working in the Prussian State Library in Berlin to gather information, she was apprehended, arrested, and interrogated, but she never admitted what she was doing. Arendt was fortunate. She might have been murdered in the cellars of the Gestapo, but she was released after eight days of interrogation. Shortly afterward, she fled from Germany. Like many German Jews, Arendt made her way to Paris, where, despite being a "stateless person," she found work with Zionist organizations. In May 1940, "enemy aliens" living in Paris (mainly German Jews) were rounded up to be sent to detention camps. She was separated from her husband and sent to the women's camp in Gurs. Arendt's good luck continued. When the Nazis marched on Paris, there was a desperate fear that Gurs would be taken over by the victorious Nazis. But there was a short period of confusion when communication broke down. The quick-witted Arendt escaped from the camp with only her toothbrush. (Many of the women who remained in Gurs were eventually sent to Nazi death camps.) She rejoined her husband in a "safe" region of France. After securing visas to enter the United States, they made the perilous journey from Vichy France through Spain to Lisbon, where they finally sailed for New York in the spring of 1941.

I have told this story of Arendt's flight from Germany, from France, and finally from Europe, for several reasons. We can readily imagine what might have happened had she been interrogated by a less sympathetic German official, had she not escaped from Gurs, had she not received a visa to enter the United States, or had she been turned back at the Spanish border (as was her close friend, Walter Benjamin, who subsequently committed suicide). These contingencies meant the difference between life and death. The radical contingency of events that so deeply marked her own personal experience influenced all her thinking. Her encounter with Nazi totalitarianism became the central experience for her thinking about politics. In 1951 she published *The Origins of Totalitarianism* – a complex book in which she set out to comprehend what had happened with the bursting forth of totalitarianism. Totalitarianism represented a complete break with tradition. Traditional political, moral, and social categories were no longer adequate to understand this new phenomenon, which she sharply distinguished from all previous forms of tyranny and dictatorship. Near the end of her study she explains why she thinks that totalitarianism represents an unprecedented radical or absolute evil.

> What totalitarian ideologies therefore aim at is not the transformation of the outside world or the transmutation of society, but the transformation of human nature itself.

The concentration camps are but laboratories where changes in human nature are tested, and their shamefulness therefore is not just the business of their inmates and those who run them according to strictly "scientific" standards; it is the concern of all men. Suffering, of which there has been always too much on earth, is not the issue, not is the number of victims. Human nature as such is at stake. (Arendt 1968: 458–9)

Totalitarianism seeks to make human beings as human beings *superfluous* – to transform them into creatures that are less than fully human.[3] In the concentration and extermination camps, there was a systematic attempt to destroy human plurality, spontaneity, individuality and natality, and freedom. More generally, she claims that totalitarianism seeks to make *all* human beings superfluous – perpetrators and victims. This is what she calls absolute or radical evil, which "confronts us with its overpowering reality and breaks down all standards we know." Mass murder, genocide, unbearable large-scale suffering by innocent people, torture, and terror have happened before in history. But it was only with totalitarianism that there was a systematic attempt to obliterate people's humanity. It is the specter of totalitarianism, in both its Nazi and Stalinist variants, that haunts and informs her understanding of politics. Totalitarianism seeks to eliminate plurality – the human condition that is the basis for action and politics. With totalitarianism there is "a much more radical liquidation of freedom as a political and as a human reality than anything we have ever witnessed before" (Arendt 1994: 408).

In order to understand what Arendt means by politics, we need to explore a network of closely interrelated concepts: debate, action, speech, plurality, natality, public space, tangible freedom, opinion, and judgment. Let me start by reflecting on what Arendt considers a truism – a truism that has all sorts of ramifications once these are teased out. She tells that "debate constitutes the very essence of political life" (Arendt 1977a: 241). We should note that, in what initially appears to be a casual remark, she does *not* say that the essence of political life is the control of the legitimate forms of violence, or even ruler-ship. Rather, the essence of politics is debate, and we will see that this has a special meaning for Arendt.

Debate itself is a form of action, and "action" is the term that Arendt uses to designate the highest form of the *vita activa* (the active life). She distinguishes action from labor and work. Labor is the activity grounded in biological necessity, and work is the activity by which we make or fabricate artificial objects. What Arendt calls action is close to what Aristotle called *praxis* – the human activity that is involved in leading an ethical and political life. Action itself is intimately related to speech. "Action and speech are so closely related because the primordial and specifically human act must at the same time contain the answer to the question asked of every newcomer: 'Who are you?' This disclosure of who somebody is, is implicit in both his words and deeds" (Arendt 1958: 178). This disclosure of who somebody is takes place in a public space where we appear to each other and debate with each other. The very condition for such action and speech is what Arendt calls *plurality*. "Action, the only activity that goes on directly between men without the intermediary of things or matter, corresponds to the human condition of plurality, to the fact that men, not Man, live on earth and inhabit the world" (Arendt 1958: 7).[4] We have already encountered the theme of plurality in our analysis of the mentality of pragmatic fallibilism. But Arendt gives plurality a distinctive political meaning. Plurality involves individuality, distinction, and equality. There is distinctiveness about each and every individual who brings to a common world a unique perspective. And this plurality is rooted in our *natality*, the capacity to begin, to intiate acton spontaneously, "To act, in its most general sense, means to take initiative, to begin . . . to set something in motion" (Arendt 1958: 177). Human beings possess this capacity by virtue of their birth. Human plurality is the basic condition of action and speech, because they take place *in between* human beings in their singularity and plurality. Action, then, is, intrinsically, political activity, and it requires the creation of those *public spaces* within which individuals can encounter each other as equals and reveal who they are.

Drawing on her interpretation of the Greek *polis*, Arendt tells us that equality – or what the Greeks called *isonomy* – exists only in the political realm where human beings encounter each other as citizens. It was only in the *polis* – in the political sphere – "that men met one another as citizens and not as private persons . . . The equality of the Greek polis, its *isonomy*, was an attribute of the polis and not of men, who received their equality by virtue of citizenship, not by virtue of birth" (Arendt 1963: 23).

Returning to the gloss on the claim that "debate is the very essence of politics," we can now see why Arendt does not think of politics as primarily involving rulership, where one person, party, or class rules over another. Rather, politics involves collective action grounded in human plurality and the equality of citizens. In this public space, individuals debate and deliberate together; they seek to persuade each other about how to conduct their public affairs. Persuasion involves open debate among equals, in which they mutually seek to clarify, test, and purify their opinions. And persuasion itself is always fallible. Debate can be contentious and *agonistic*; it does not necessarily result in, or presuppose, consensus. But politics requires a commitment to persuasion – and when we fail to persuade, we must at least agree on fair procedures for making decisions.

We can deepen our understanding of what Arendt means by politics by seeing how she integrates the concepts of public tangible freedom and the type of power that spontaneously emerges when citizens act together. Referring to the *philosophes* of the Enlightenment, whose importance, she says, lies in their shrewd insight into the public character of freedom, Arendt tells us:

> Their public freedom was not an inner realm into which men might escape at will from the pressures of the world, nor was it the *liberum arbitrium* which makes the will choose between alternatives. Freedom for them could exist only in public; it was a tangible, worldly reality, something created by men to be enjoyed by men rather than a gift or capacity, it was the man-made public space or marketplace which antiquity had known as the area where freedom appears and becomes visible to all. (Arendt 1963: 120–1)

Public freedom must be sharply distinguished from liberty. Liberty is always liberation *from* something, whether it is liberation *from* poverty, or *from* oppressive rulers, tyrants, and dictators. Liberty is a *necessary* condition for freedom, but not a *sufficient* condition. Freedom is a positive political *achievement* of individuals acting together. And this tangible worldly freedom exists only as long as citizens deliberate, debate, and act together. The distinction between liberty and freedom is one of Arendt's most important, enduring, and relevant political insights. Over and over again – especially after the fall of communism in 1989 – we have to learn the painful lesson that liberation from oppressive leaders is not sufficient to bring about public freedom. One of the greatest disasters of the "political rhetoric" justifying the military invasion of Iraq is the (false) belief that liberation from the tyrannical oppression of Saddam Hussein would immediately initiate public freedom in Iraq and in the entire Middle East. This is a dangerous illusion. Public freedom requires far more than formal elections. It requires the cultivation of those practices such that individuals debate and deliberate together. It is only with the creation of such spaces that worldly freedom flourishes.

Corresponding to this idea of tangible public freedom, Arendt develops her distinctive concept of political power. She criticizes the traditional idea of power, where power is understood as the domination of an individual or a group *over* other individuals or groups. Power, which she distinguishes from strength, force, authority, and violence, arises and grows spontaneously through participation of citizens. Power is not to be understood in a vertical fashion, where power means control or domination *over* some individual or group. It is a *horizontal* concept – power springs up when individuals act together.[5]

> [P]ower comes into being only if and when men join themselves together for the purpose of action, and it will disappear when for whatever reason, they disperse and desert one another. Hence binding and promising, combining and covenanting are the means by which power is kept in existence; where and when men succeed in keeping intact the power which sprang up between them during the course of any particular act or deed, they are already in the process of foundation, of constituting a stable worldly structure to house, as it were, their combined power of action. (Arendt 1963: 174)

So power, like public freedom, plurality, natality, action, speech, and debate, is woven into the fabric of Arendt's understanding of politics.

Before turning to the question of how Arendt integrates her understanding of opinion and judgment into her conception of politics, I want to address an often-repeated criticism of her concept of politics. Some critics argue that Arendt bases her understanding of politics upon an idealized conception of the Greek *polis* that does not correspond even to the realities of ancient Greek life. Furthermore, whatever the merits of this conception of politics, it is not relevant to the complexities and harsh realities of contemporary politics and mass democratic societies. I think it is false to suggest that Arendt was interested primarily in an imagined "golden era" of the Greek city-state. There is nothing nostalgic or sentimental about her thinking. As I have already insisted, Arendt's lifelong concern with politics had its roots in her insight that totalitarianism sought to destroy the very possibility of politics, freedom, and, consequently, our humanity. But, what is even more important, Arendt's primary intention is to reclaim a *human potentiality*, one that is rooted in our natality and has been manifested at different times in radically different historical circumstances. This is not a fanciful utopian possibility. It has been *actualized* in different historical settings in the modern age. She calls this "the lost treasure of the revolutionary spirit."

> The history of revolutions – from the summer of 1776 in Philadelphia and the summer of 1789 in Paris to the autumn in Budapest – which politically spells the innermost story of the modern age, and could be told in a parable as a tale of an age-old treasure which, under the most varied circumstances, appears abruptly, unexpectedly, and disappears again, under different mysterious conditions, as though it were a fata morgana. (Arendt 1977a: 5)

Arendt's favorite example of politics – and her most extended analysis – is the American Revolution. In speaking of the American Revolution, she is referring to the events that began in 1776 with the Declaration of

Independence and culminated with the writing and adoption of the Constitution. Indeed, it is the deliberation, debates, compromises, and ultimate success in adopting the Constitution that epitomizes the tangible worldly freedom that she describes. This is a historically concrete example of the creation of public spaces in which power arises through collective action of individuals. The Constitution lays the foundation for those institutions that house and preserve this freedom.

> [T]he course of the American revolution tells an unforgettable story and is apt to teach a unique lesson: for this revolution did not break out but was made by men in common deliberation and on the strength of mutual pledges. The principle which came to light during those fateful years when foundations were laid – not by the strength of one architect but by the combined power of the many – was the interconnected principle of mutual promise and common deliberation; and the event itself decided indeed, as Hamilton had insisted, that men "are really capable . . . of establishing good government from reflection and choice," that they are not "forever destined to depend for their political constitutions on accident and force." (Arendt 1963: 215)

Arendt's characterization of politics captures what is vital for a flourishing democratic politics. She warns about the danger of forgetfulness of this treasure. So much of our chatter about democratic politics today is so heavily encrusted with clichés that we too easily forget this vital core. Arendt would be sharply critical of the post-9/11 absolutist discourse of good and evil. Any appeal to absolutes in politics corrupts and destroys politics. When absolutes – whether absolute goodness or absolute evil – enter into politics, they can all too easily and ineluctably lead to violence. And for Arendt, it is violence that destroys politics. This is a lesson that is portrayed with the utmost vividness by poets and novelists. In her discussion of Melville's *Billy Budd* and Dostoevsky's *Grand Inquisitor* in *On Revolution*, she argues that "the absolute spells doom to everyone when it is introduced into the political realm" (1963: 79). Arendt agrees with the pragmatists that tough moral and political choices may require choosing the lesser evil. It is the *absolutizing* of evil that is dangerous. This becomes even clearer in Arendt's discussion of the role of opinion and judgment in politics.

Forming, testing, and clarifying opinions takes place in political debate. What Arendt means by opinion has little to do what pollsters and politicians call opinions. Individuals do not simply "have" opinions, they *form* opinions. The formation of opinions requires what Arendt calls "representative thinking."

> I form an opinion by considering a given issue from different viewpoints, by making present to my mind the standpoints of those who are absent; that is, I represent them ... The more people's standpoints that I have present in my mind while I am pondering a given issue, and the better I can imagine how I would feel and think if I were in their place, the stronger will be my capacity for representative thinking and the more valid my final conclusions, my opinion. (Arendt 1977a: 241)

Consequently, the formation of opinion is an *achievement* that requires political representative thinking. The formation of opinions is not a private activity performed by a solitary thinker. Opinions can be tested and enlarged only when there is a genuine encounter – even a clash – with differing opinions in the public spaces of debate among equals.

> Opinions ... never belong to groups but exclusively to individuals, who "exert their reason coolly and freely," and no

multitude, be it the multitude of a part or of the whole of society, will ever be capable of forming an opinion. Opinions will rise wherever men communicate freely with one another and have the right to make their views public, but these views in their endless variety seem to stand also in need of purification and representation. (Arendt 1963: 229)

The formation and refining of opinions through public testing and debate enable us to understand the type of judging that Arendt takes to be essential for politics. "Judging," Arendt tells us, "is one, if not the most, important activity in which this sharing-the-world-with-others comes to pass." Drawing her inspiration from her interpretation of Kant's analysis of reflective judgment, she tells us that judging requires an "enlarged mentality" that enables one to "think in the place of everybody else." "The judging person, as Kant says quite beautifully, can only 'woo the consent of everyone else' in the hope of coming to an agreement with him eventually" (Arendt 1977a: 222). This wooing, this persuasion, is essential for politics. There is no guarantee that we will succeed in this wooing, and there is no guarantee that we will come to agreement with our fellow citizens. There may be irreconcilable conflicts in the clash of opinions. But participants must be committed to the *potential* for agreement with others. And if we fail to achieve agreement in our judgments, then we must at least agree on fair procedures for making decisions – procedures that protect the rights of minorities. The key elements of Arendt's conception of political judgment are summed up in the following passage:

> The power of judgment rests on a potential agreement with others, and the thinking process which is active in judging something is not, like the thought process of pure reasoning, a dialogue between me and myself, but finds itself always and primarily, even if I am quite alone in making up

my mind, in an anticipated communication with others with whom I know I must finally come to some agreement. From this potential agreement judgment derives its specific validity. This means, on the one hand, that such judgment must liberate itself from the "subjective private conditions," that is, from the idiosyncrasies which naturally determine the outlook of each individual in his privacy and are legitimate as long as they are only privately held opinions, but which are not fit to enter the market place, and lack all validity in the public realm. And this enlarged way of thinking, which as judgment knows how to transcend its own individual limitations, on the other hand, cannot function in strict isolation or solitude; it needs the presence of others "in whose place" it must think, whose perspectives it must take into consideration, and without whom it never has the opportunity to operate at all. (Arendt 1977a: 220–1)

We can start with any of the strands that are woven into Arendt's political thinking – debate, action, speech, plurality, natality, public space, tangible public freedom, power, opinion, and judgment – and we discover that they lead to, and reinforce, a compelling vision of what constitutes politics. *There is no place for absolutes in politics.* The lesson that Arendt teaches us is the same lesson that the pragmatic thinkers sought to teach us in their response to American Civil War – that the mentality that appeals to absolutes and rigid certainties can lead to violence.

Arendt had an acute sense of the powerful tendencies in modern society to undermine, distort, and suppress politics. But she never gave up her belief in the power of the "revolutionary spirit." In her own lifetime, she saw it manifested in the Budapest uprising of 1956 and in the early Civil Rights movement in the United States. And if she had lived to witness the emergence of the political movements that led to the downfall of communism in Eastern and Central Europe, she would have cited them as further evidence of the power of the revolutionary spirit – the power that springs forth when individuals act together. (Leaders of these movements, such as Adam Michnik in Poland, drew their inspiration from the political writings of Arendt.) Like Jefferson, Arendt emphasized the importance of "elementary republics," or what she called "councils," in keeping alive democratic politics.

> The councils say: We want to participate, we want to debate, we want to make our voices heard in public, and we want to have a possibility to determine the political course of our country. Since the country is too big for all of us to come together and determine our fate, we need a number of public spaces within it. The booth in which we deposit our ballots is unquestionably too small, for this booth has room for only one. The parties are completely unsuitable; there we are, most of us, nothing but a manipulated electorate. But if only ten of us are sitting around a table, each expressing his opinion, each hearing the opinion of others, then a rational formation of opinion can take place through the exchange of opinions. (Arendt 1972: 233)

There is a significant overlap between Arendt's conception of politics and the pragmatists' – especially Dewey's and Mead's – conception of democracy. Dewey, like Arendt, sees that one of the most serious threats to democracy is the "eclipse of the public." Dewey too thought that a healthy democracy, even in complex industrial and technological societies, demands creation of public spaces where individuals can debate together. In response to the criticism that his faith in democracy was utopian, Dewey responded in words that reinforce what we learn from Arendt:

> I have been accused more than once and from opposed quarters of an undue, a utopian, faith in intelligence and in

education as a correlate of intelligence. At all events, I did not invent this faith. I acquired it from my surroundings as far as those surroundings were animated by the democratic spirit. For what is the faith in democracy, in the role of consultation, of conference, of persuasion, of discussion, in the formation of public opinion, which in the long run is self-corrective, except faith in the capacity of the intelligence of the common man to respond with commonsense to the free play of facts and ideas which are secured by effective guarantees of free inquiry, free assembly and free communication? (Dewey 1988: 227)[6]

What Dewey wrote in 1939 is even more urgent today. "We have to re-create by deliberate and determined endeavor the kind of democracy which in its origin one hundred and fifty years ago was largely a product of a fortunate combination of men and circumstances." And he goes on to declare:

If I emphasize that the task can be accomplished only by inventive effort and creative activity, it is in part because the depth of the present crisis is due in considerable part to the fact that for a long period we acted as if democracy were something that perpetuated itself automatically ... We acted as if democracy were something that took place mainly at Washington or Albany – or some other state capital – under the impetus of what happened when men and women went to the polls once a year or so.... We can escape from this external way of thinking only as we realize in thought and act that democracy is a *personal way* of individual life; that it signifies the possession and continual use of certain attitudes, forming personal character and determining desire and purpose in all the relations of life. (Dewey 1988: 225–6)

The reason why I think that these reflections on democratic politics are so important and relevant for us today is because they emphasize what is required to *revitalize* "really existing" large-scale democratic societies. Neither Arendt nor the pragmatists offer blueprints for what is to be done. And there are many issues concerning the structure and functions of democratic law and institutions that they neglect. Both Arendt and the pragmatists are aware of the subtle and strong forces in modern life that undermine and distort democratic politics. But they remind us of what is vital for the flourishing of democratic politics, and they emphasize that creating those public spaces in which tangible freedom flourishes is always "a task before us." They teach us that introducing absolutes, alleged moral certainties, and rigid simplistic dichotomies of good and evil *corrupt* democratic politics.

But still it may be asked how these reflections on democratic politics bear on our current situation. What lessons can we learn from them? Let me review some of the points that I have already made – and develop them further. The most important point is to understand why the introduction of absolutes – and especially demonizing one's enemies as absolutely evil – distorts and corrupts politics. To speak in this way, to speak about the "evil ones," "the servants of evil," "the axis of evil" – as Bush frequently does – may be highly successful in playing on people's fears and anxieties, but it blocks serious deliberation and diplomacy. It is used to "justify" risky military interventions and to *trump* serious consideration of alternatives in responding to real dangers. It rules out the possibility of the type of democratic discussion wherein dissenting views are respected and carefully evaluated. It stifles serious inquiry about complex issues that need to be carefully analyzed, investigated, and debated. Ron Suskind reports a chilling conversation with Bruce Bartlett, a domestic policy advisor to Ronald Reagan and a treasury official under the first President Bush. Speaking about George W. Bush, Bartlett said: "He truly believes he's on a mission from God.

Absolute faith overwhelms a need for analysis. The whole thing about faith is to believe things for which there is no empirical evidence" (Suskind 2004: 46). Unfortunately, many Christian conservatives do believe that Bush is executing God's will. Suskind goes on to tell us that already in the summer of 2001 "a cluster of particularly vivid qualities was shaping George W. Bush's White House ...: a disdain for contemplation or deliberation, an embrace of decisiveness, a retreat from empiricism, a sometimes bullying impatience with doubters and even friendly questioners. Already Bush was saying, Have faith in me and my decisions, and you'll be rewarded. All through the White House, people were channeling the boss. He didn't second-guess himself; why should they?" (Suskind 2004: 49). Paul O'Neill, who was asked to resign as Bush's Secretary of the Treasury, told Suskind: "If you operate in a certain way – by saying this is how I want to justify what I've decided to do, and I don't care how you pull it off – you guarantee that you'll get faulty, one-sided information" (Suskind 2004: 51). The combination of Bush's faith-based self-assurance and his appeal to his "gut instincts" is not exactly exemplary of the virtues of democratic deliberation and debate. But Bush's character and personality are *not* the primary issue; rather, it is the *mentality* he exhibits that is so scary.

When Bob Woodward interviewed Bush for his book *Bush at War*, Bush told Woodward: "There is no doubt in my mind we're doing the right thing. Not one doubt." And when Woodward asked him whether he had consulted his father on the war in Iraq, Bush replied, "He is the wrong father to appeal to in terms of strength. There is a higher power I appeal to" (quoted in Schlesinger 2004: 35). One does not have to doubt the sincerity of Bush's faith or mock his religious beliefs, but such an appeal to the Almighty in making *political* decisions is antithetical to the spirit of democratic politics, debate, and deliberation. Because the

world of political action always involves unforeseen consequences, *reasoned doubt* is always appropriate when making
momentous decisions. But this is a president who doesn't
admit to having made any significant mistakes.

Reflection on the concrete meaning of democratic politics and public freedom might also forestall reliance on
clichés and empty rhetoric. In his Second Inaugural
Address and his State of the Union address, Bush reiterated the words "freedom," "liberty," and "democracy" over
and over again – as if they constituted an incantation or
mantra. Such ritual occasions are not ideal opportunities
for analytical finesse. But one can't help but draw the conclusion that all this talk about our mission to spread
freedom and democracy throughout the world is intended
to help us forget that the original justification of the Iraq
war was the presumed "imminent threat" of Saddam's
weapons of mass destruction. The use of such "uplifting"
rhetoric suffers from double-edged dangers. It can easily
be heard as hypocritical, empty rhetoric or a screen with
which to justify new risky military interventions – as we
bring freedom and democracy to the rest of the world.

Earlier I mentioned Arendt's important distinction
between liberty and freedom, where liberty means "liberty
from," and freedom means the *achievement* of public tangible freedom in the public spaces that arise when individuals act and deliberate together. The reason why I believe
her distinction to be so relevant today is because much of
the administration's rhetoric about overthrowing Saddam
Hussein suggested that liberation from this ruthless dictator would immediately lead to the flourishing of freedom
and democracy in Iraq. Many influential neo-cons spoke as
if American soldiers would be embraced as the great liber-
ators of the Iraqi people. And they were convinced that
they were right, because this is what they wanted to hear
(and were told) by their Iraqi friends. It has become

painfully clear that the Bush government had no detailed plans for what to do after the military "victory," and no expectation of the widespread deadly insurrection that has taken place. The president and his advisors believed that once the Iraqi people were liberated *from* Saddam Hussein, the transition to democracy would be relatively straightforward and smooth. (And if they did not really believe this, they certainly did not reveal their doubts to the American public.) The president and his cabinet officers still refuse to admit that they made any mistakes; that they made fallible judgments that turned out to be wrong.

I also want to emphasize a point that I made earlier when describing the pragmatic mentality. I indicated that reasonable people can and do disagree. Pragmatic fallibilism does not *dictate* substantive conclusions and decisions; rather, it is primarily concerned with *how* these decisions are reached, discussed, and debated. Let me illustrate this with reference to some of the public debates that actually took place (outside the administration) *before* the military intervention in Iraq. Personally, I – like many other Americans – strongly opposed this military intervention. I did not subscribe to the idea of a preemptive or, more accurately, *preventive* war. I saw this as a radical change in American foreign policy – a change that was unjustified. I did believe that Saddam Hussein had chemical and biological weapons – primarily because he had already used chemical weapons against the Kurds. But I did not think that he posed an "imminent threat" to the United States. I was dubious about the alleged evidence of his possession of nuclear weapons. I favored a strong policy of containment and deterrence – isolating Saddam Hussein. Ironically – although no one knew it at the time – this policy had been working, because he had destroyed whatever weapons of mass destruction he possessed. Even when this became clear, the president and vice-president went on reassuring us that WMD would be discovered. I felt that the unilateral policy that the US was following would have long-range damaging consequences in undermining multi-lateral cooperation with our allies. I did not think that there was any substantial evidence linking Hussein to Al-Qaeda and the attack on the World Trade Center. Furthermore, given Hussein's secularism and bin Ladin's fanatical Islamic fundamentalism, I did not think that it made any sense to link them together in the "War on Terror." But the primary reason why I opposed the war was because I was convinced that the US government was completely in the dark about what would happen in Iraq after the overthrow of Saddam Hussein. There was no understanding of the chaos and the forces that would be unleashed in Iraq.

But there were other persons whom I respected who argued for military intervention. They argued that Hussein was more than just a ruthless dictator; that he was prepared to commit genocide against his own population, and that he was ruthless in stifling any dissent and in eliminating anyone who opposed him. They argued that no nation should get away with flouting so many United Nations resolutions, and that the US had made an effort to work through the United Nations and to convince its allies to join in a military intervention. But there had come a point when it needed to exercise its decisive leadership. As long as Hussein was in power, there would never be any solution to the problems in the Middle East. Hussein used Scud missiles against Israel in the First Gulf War, and there was no reason to believe that he might not do so again – and with more effectiveness. Some argued that the military intervention was not really a new initiative, but would complete the unfinished First Gulf War. And although there were many uncertainties about what would happen after the fall of Hussein, it certainly could not be worse than living under his ruthless dictatorship.

In a democracy, there ought to be ample opportunity for the full expression of opinions pro and con when the nation is considering a momentous decision involving war. Even after the arguments pro and con are aired, there must be fair democratic procedures for making controversial decisions. But responsible defenders of military intervention did *not* appeal to religious faith, did *not* appeal to absolutes, did *not* assert their moral certainty, did *not* seek to justify the war as an American "crusade" against evil.[7] Even though I remain convinced that the reasons against the war were far stronger than those offered in support of war, I certainly do not want to deny that many of those who advocated going to war in Iraq offered good reasons to warrant their position. A democracy thrives on the conflict of opinions. Pragmatic fallibilism encourages such conflict, but it is wary of any attempt to displace the healthy conflict of opinions with appeals to absolutes, moral certainty, and stark moralistic dichotomies of good and evil.

In introducing my discussion of democratic politics, I began with Arendt's declaration that "debate constitutes the very essence of political life." I did so because drawing out the meaning and consequences of this claim enables us understand why appeals to absolutes about good and evil corrupt democratic politics. But, of course, there are other, competing conceptions of politics. One of the most controversial is Carl Schmitt's characterization of "the political." Carl Schmitt was a German jurist and political theorist who died in 1985 at the age of 96. His career spanned the First World War, the collapse of the Weimar Republic, the rise of Hitler, and the Second World War. Because he was an enthusiastic supporter of Hitler, a vicious anti-Semite, and a relentless critic of liberalism, pluralism, and parliamentary democracy, he has been severely criticized and condemned. But there are a growing number of thinkers – conservatives and even left intellectuals – who claim that Schmitt is one of the most important political theorists of the twentieth century.

Schmitt – especially in his pre-Nazi writings – articulated a view of politics that captures something important about "really existing politics." The best introduction to Schmitt's thought is *The Concept of the Political*. It first appeared as a journal article in 1927 (the same year that Dewey published *The Public and its Problems*) and was expanded as a short book, which he revised several times. Schmitt raises the same question that Arendt asks: What is politics? Or, more accurately, What is the political? In seeking to clarify "the political" (*das Politische*) he focuses on the criterion for demarcating what is distinctive about politics. He emphatically tells us: "The specific political distinction to which political actions and motives can be reduced is that between friend and enemy" (Schmitt 1995: 26). And by an "enemy" he means a *public* adversary. Unless there is a clearly defined enemy, unless there is group that we identify as strange and alien, then, strictly speaking, there is *no* politics. Politics does not shun or seek to avoid conflict. It thrives on conflict. Unlike Arendt, Schmitt does not think that the violence of war is a threat to politics. "War is neither the aim nor the purpose nor even the very content of politics. But as an ever present possibility it is the leading presupposition which determines in a characteristic way human action and thinking and thereby creates a specifically political behavior" (Schmitt 1995: 34). Those who think that there can be politics without conflict, struggle, and even war are naïve. Worse than that, they fail to realize that they are seeking to destroy and eliminate politics. According to Schmitt, liberalism seeks to bring about the end of politics.[8] Liberalism advances the "fiction" that the state is neutral, that its primary function is to protect individual rights and to develop political institutions (e.g., parliaments and congresses) that enable and promote compromises and the peaceful resolution of conflicts under the rule of a neutral law. He even claims that there is "absolutely no liberal politics, only a liberal critique of politics." Although Schmitt distinguishes the different domains of morality, religion, aesthetics, and politics, everything is *potentially* political, because in exceptional circumstances any domain can become political if it is employed to distinguish friend from enemy. We find here one of the many disturbing tensions in Schmitt's thinking. He sharply distinguishes morality, based on the distinction between good and evil, from politics, based on the sharp distinction between friend and enemy. Even though morality can be *used* to define the political enemy, Schmitt thoroughly condemns a universalistic moral humanism. When the enemy is subsumed under the universal moral categories of good and evil, the enemy is turned into an inhuman monster that must be totally annihilated. Such a universalistic moralism is hypocritically used to "justify" *total war*, which demands the complete annihilation of the foe. Schmitt draws a distinction between the *enemy* as one's political adversary and the *foe* – those whom we condemn as morally evil and seek to annihilate. An enemy need not be considered to be morally evil. Consequently, wars against enemies are limited. They are won when the enemy is defeated. Wars against foes are *total* wars; they are won only when the foe is completely annihilated. Schmitt's rhetoric about "the political" is saturated with strong moral and religious evaluations. (For his damning critique of the "concept of humanity" in politics, see Schmitt 1995: 54.)

Schmitt draws an extremely important conclusion from this understanding of the political. Every political group requires a sovereign, who has the task of making *decisions* in exceptional or extreme circumstances. *And it is the sovereign who decides whether a situation is exceptional.* From Schmitt's perspective, debate is certainly not the essence of politics. Debate, deliberation, and persuasion obscure what is essential for politics – firm sovereign decisions for dealing with political enemies. Sovereigns may *pretend* that they are making fundamental decisions in the name of some "higher principle" or that they are following proper legal and political procedures, but this should not disguise the fact that such decisions are ungrounded; they are solely the sovereign's decisions. There is no higher appeal than the sovereign's decision.

With liberalism there is a greater fear of making and carrying out these firm sovereign decisions than there is of one's enemies. Liberals fail to acknowledge that political enmity can never be eliminated *completely*. Enmity is a basic *existential* feature of human beings, and if we ignore or obscure it, then we will be thoroughly naïve about the essential character of real politics.[9] There is no way of avoiding sovereign decisions, and no way of eliminating the existential enmity that is the basis for the political distinction between friend and enemy.

One of the lively debates about Schmitt's conception of the political concerns how, precisely, we are to understand the main thrust of what he is claiming. Is he concerned primarily with developing a realistic conception of how politics actually works? Or is he concerned to tell us what "real" politics *ought* to be? He seems to want to do both. He argues that the opposition between friend and enemy has always characterized real politics, although – in the past – there have been very "civilized" forms of politics and war. He also claims that the new type of *total war* that emerged in the twentieth century is a consequence of a false universal humanism. He strongly objects to all those tendencies (e.g. liberalism and technology) in modernity that "depoliticize" politics. Consequently, if we are ruthlessly honest, we *ought* to avoid liberal hypocrisy, we *ought* to recognize that the friend/enemy dichotomy defines "the political," and we *ought* to recognize that sovereigns define those exceptional circumstances that call for firm decisions. We should not be sentimental about the need for exceptional sovereign decisions. It is the exceptions to so-called normal everyday politics that bring out the *true* character of politics.

One of the reasons why Schmitt has been receiving so much attention lately is because he appears to have put his finger on a key feature of modern politics. One can tell a story of politics since the First World War that "fits" Schmitt's friend/enemy dichotomy. It is grist for Schmitt's mill that the attempts to create institutions to contain and regulate political enmity and prevent wars (the League of Nations and the United Nations) have failed to do so. With the end of the Cold War, politics in the Schmittian sense seemed to flounder. But with 9/11, the new "War on Terror" created a strong new sense of political identity and purpose – at least for the United States. Now there is presumably a clear sense of political friend and enemy. The president of the United States frequently speaks of those who are *with us* and those who are *against us* in the "War on Terror." Our political identity is sharpened against this new enemy – we are the "lovers and defenders of freedom and democracy." And we can even see the role of the sovereign decision in exceptional circumstances. After all, it was President Bush who made the sovereign decision to go to war in Iraq. (It should be noted, however, that a "War on Terror" in the name of universal human freedom fits Schmitt's description of disastrous *total war*.) Most of the reasons advanced for going to war in Iraq have now been discredited. But from a Schmittian perspective, this is not really relevant, because sovereign decisions are *never* really justified by reasons. And the religious and moral talk of good and evil is best understood as a *political* means for distinguishing ourselves from our enemies.

There is an extremely dark underside to this Schmittian conception of politics. There are, of course, *real* enemies that nations must fight. There is nothing fictitious about the existence of the Al-Qaeda. But what is really important for Schmitt is the *construction* of an enemy in order to define one's political identity. That is precisely what the United States has done; it has *constructed* an all-inclusive, threatening enemy – "the servants of Evil." And in constructing this enemy, it has played on and manipulated people's fears and anxieties. Manipulating fear is one of the most powerful political weapons for defining the enemy. On the one hand, Schmitt emphasizes the importance for politics of identifying an enemy; on the other hand, he condemns the "hypocritical" moralism of those seeking complete annihilation of the enemy.

Some commentators have thought of Schmitt as a contemporary Thomas Hobbes. Although Schmitt admires Hobbes, he is actually a severe critic of Hobbes, because he claims that Hobbes laid the foundations for modern liberalism. Hobbes, like Schmitt, does think that enmity, or belligerence, is the natural condition of human beings. But Hobbes's *Leviathan* is intended to show how this belligerence can be controlled and contained by creating a "mortal god" – a sovereign to guarantee security. But, according to Schmitt, we cannot and should not pacify political enmity. Hobbes, then, is no better than those liberals who claim that the aim of politics is to seek peace and security. Schmitt's political-theological imperative is "Fight Thy Enemy."

There is a deep irony in applying Schmittian principles to the current political situation in the United States. We presumably fought the war in Iraq in the name of the liberal democratic principles that Schmitt scorns and finds contemptible. We keep hearing about the importance of freedom and the need to help Iraq and the Middle East to become genuine democracies. From Schmitt's perspective this is hypocritical. For Schmitt, the United States represents the *worst* form of liberalism – a liberalism that pretends to be democratic, universalistic, and humanitarian, but is actually responsible for bringing about total war. William E. Scheuerman notes that Schmitt's anti-Americanism is so extreme that he claims that the United States – "as that world power which systematically synthesizes awesome military power with liberal universalism ... now menaces humanity to a greater degree than recent totalitarian dictatorships" (Scheuerman 2004: 545).[10]

But I do think that there is an important lesson to be learned from Schmitt – although it is not the lesson he intended. There is a real clash between the democratic politics that I have described and the Schmittian conception of politics. Schmitt claims that liberalism, when unmasked, is really anti-democratic. But Schmitt is no friend of democracy. If we take Schmitt seriously, then debate, deliberation, persuasion, public spaces, and public tangible freedom are not only irrelevant to politics; they obscure the real character of politics. The more we act on Schmittian principles, the more we *undermine* democratic politics.

The basic issue today is not whether we have real enemies or whether it is necessary to fight these enemies, but rather how we *think* and *act* in extreme situations. I have already cited Sidney Hook's remark: "Realization of the evil men can do and have done to men is integral to any intelligent appraisal of human history." But we can face these concrete specific evils, and even make hard choices and decisions, without accepting the Schmittian claim that enmity is the basic existential condition of human beings. And we must be wary of sliding into a mode of thinking and acting that is all too ready to sacrifice democratic practices and principles for a specious "tough-minded" political realism. Our task today is to *reinvigorate* democracy – not to abandon it in the name of Schmittian politics.

5

Evil and the Corruption
of Religion

The popular post-9/11 discourse about good and evil *corrupts* religion. There is no doubt that the religious right in the United States has been exerting a growing influence on American politics. But we must not identify religion with the religious right – or with what has been called the "New Christian Right." We must not allow any denomination, group, or coalition of religious groups to "steal" the mantle of religion and to determine what is evil. In my introduction, I indicated that at the heart of the world religions – including Judaism, Christianity, and Islam – the concern with good and evil has been central. Every religion seeks to characterize what is good and evil – and how we are to combat the evil that lies within us and within the world. From the perspective of monotheistic religions, it is God who is the source and ground of our morality – the basis for distinguishing good and evil. Many modern thinkers have maintained that we do not have to appeal to religion to ground our morality. Kant was a Christian believer who has had a great influence on Protestant theology and religious thought. Nevertheless, he categorically asserts "for its own sake morality does not need religion at all ... by virtue of pure practical reason it is self-sufficient" (Kant 1960: 3). But this is not what many ordinary religious persons believe; on the contrary, they believe that religious faith grounds morality and the knowledge of good and evil.

When we examine the world religions, we discover that in every great religious tradition there has been an ongoing discussion and debate about the very meaning of good and evil. Living religious traditions are not monolithic. There really is no such thing as *the* religious understanding of good and evil. There is no such thing as *the* Christian, *the* Jewish, or *the* Islamic conception of good and evil. And this is just as true for the entire range of living religious traditions. Plurality and diversity are not threats to religious traditions; they are what keep religious traditions alive. Religious concepts of good and evil are *essentially contested concepts*. To say that good and evil are essentially contested is not to say, "Anything goes." On the contrary, it means that one is under an obligation to explain and justify one's distinctive religious understanding of good and evil. There is a great religious tradition of *faith seeking understanding*. And this seeking involves questioning, thinking, and struggling to clarify and deepen one's faith. Alasdair Macintyre gives us one of the best succinct definitions of a tradition – including a religious tradition. He tells us that "a tradition not only embodies the narrative of an argument, but is recovered by the argumentative retelling of that narrative which will itself be in conflict with other argumentative retellings" (Macintyre 1977: 461). This applies to the retelling of competing conceptions of good and evil. Consequently, we betray what is best in a living religious tradition when we identify religion with uncritical dogmatism or fanaticism. When someone claims that he knows what evil is because he is a religious believer, and that no further explanation or justification is needed, he is guilty of the sin of pride.

What I find so objectionable about the post-9/11 talk of good and evil is this arrogance. To speak about evil as if its meaning were perfectly clear, as if it needed no further commentary or discussion, is dangerous. "Evil" tends to be used in an excessively vague and permissive manner in order to condemn whatever one finds abhorrent. One doesn't have to *think*, because presumably the meaning of evil is self-evident. Furthermore, "evil" is used in a highly selective and self-serving manner. Among religious and nonreligious ethicists, torture is has been considered to be *intrinsically* evil. There have been an increasing number of reliable reports about the widespread use of torture and deliberate humiliation not only at Abu Ghraib, but throughout Iraq.[1] And the Red Cross has reported that practices "tantamount to torture" have taken place at prison in Guantánamo Bay. But somehow these don't count as evil. I do not know of a single statement by a member of the current United States administration who has condemned these practices as *evil*.

Andrew Sullivan, an outstanding journalist, who has been a strong and articulate defender of the US military intervention in Iraq, has eloquently expressed his outrage about the atrocities committed by Americans "in plain sight."

> But in a democracy, the responsibility [for the torture and humiliation of prisoners] is also wider. Did those of us who fought so passionately for a ruthless war against terrorists give an unwitting green light to these abuses? Were we naïve in believing that characterizing complex conflicts from Afghanistan to Iraq as a single simple war against "evil" might not filter down and lead to decisions that could dehumanize the enemy and lead to abuse? Did our conviction of our own rightness in this struggle make it hard for us to acknowledge when that good cause had become endangered? I fear the answer to each of these questions is yes . . . . Advocates of the war, especially those allied with the administration, kept relatively quiet, or attempted to belittle what

had gone on, or made facile arguments that such things always occur in wartime. But it seems to me that those of us who are most committed to the Iraq intervention should be the most vociferous in highlighting these excrescences. Getting rid of this cancer within the system is essential to winning this war. (Sullivan 2005: 11)

It is a shame that the administration does not share Sullivan's sense of outrage. Despite loose talk about "taking responsibility" for what happened at Abu Ghraib, these seem to be empty, meaningless words, because no important civilian or military officer has been fired or removed from office. On the contrary, those who helped to clear the way for such abuses have been rewarded. "The man who paved the way for the torture of prisoners is to be entrusted with safeguarding the civil rights of Americans. It is astonishing that he has been nominated, and even more astonishing that he will almost certainly be confirmed" (Sullivan 2005: 11).[2]

Why has this happened? Why have Bush and his cohorts been so reluctant to face up to this blatant evil? Of course, there are political reasons for downplaying its significance, for seeing it as the actions of a few "bad apples." The international publicity given to the abuses at Abu Ghraib is a source of embarrassment to the US administration. But another important factor is that acknowledging that Americans commit atrocities doesn't fit with the "moral" universe *constructed* by this administration. After all, we are the good guys who are dedicated to spreading democracy and freedom, and we are fighting the bad guys – the evil ones. In a world where there is a stark black-and-white opposition between good and evil, good guys do not commit evil atrocities. And for those who appeal to the New Testament for moral guidance, they might remember Paul's admonition: "Do not repay anyone evil for evil. . . . Be not overcome by evil, but over-come evil with good."

In order to explain why I think that the careless way in which "evil" is being used today has a corrupting effect on religion, I want to explore a number of related issues. To begin, I want to consider the distinction between the "religious" and the "secular." The uses of "religious" and "secular" have become so familiar that we rarely stop to think about the meaning of these terms. Etymologically, "secular" is a word that is derived from the medieval Latin *saeculum*, which means primarily "world." As José Casanova tells us, in medieval Canon Law, "secularization refers to the legal (canonical process) whereby a 'religious' person left the cloister to return to the 'world' and its temptations, becoming a 'secular' person. Canonically, priests could be both 'religious' and 'secular.' Those priests who decided to withdraw from the world (*saeculum*) to dedicate themselves to a life of perfection formed the religious clergy. Those persons who lived in the world formed the secular clergy" (Casanova 1994: 13). What is noteworthy about this early meaning of "secular" is that, although there is a distinction between religious persons living within the walls of a cloister and those living outside in the world (*saeculum*), nevertheless, a religious person could be *both* religious and secular. A Christian priest living in the world (*saeculum*) was (and is) a secular priest. As Casanova points out, "the structured division of 'this world' into two separate spheres, 'religious' and 'secular,' has to be distinguished and kept separate from another division: that between 'this world' and 'the other world'" (Casanova 1994: 14). In pre-modern Western Christendom, however, there are not two worlds, but three. There is the other world (heaven) and this world (earth). But this world is itself divided into the religious world (the Church) and the secular world proper (the *saeculum*). The Church is situated in the middle of this double, dualist system of classification as the mediator between this world (earth) and the other world (heaven), as well as between the religious and the secular spheres in this world. This "spatialized" picture is an idealization, because there were always tensions and disputes about the precise boundaries between the religious and the secular.

It is against this background that we can understand what secularization as a historical process means.

> Secularization as a concept refers to the actual historical process whereby this dualist system within "this world" and the sacramental structures of mediation between this world and the other world progressively break down until the entire medieval system of classification disappears, to be replaced by new systems of spatial structuration of the spheres. Max Weber's expressive image of the breaking of the monastery walls remains perhaps the best graphic description of this radical spatial restructuration. The wall separating the religious and the secular realms within "this world" breaks down. The separation between "this world" and "the other world," for the time being at least remains. But from now on, there will be only one single "this world," the secular one, within which religion will have to find its own place. If before, it was the religious realm which appeared to be the all-encompassing reality within which the secular realm found its proper place, now the secular sphere will be the all-encompassing reality, to which the religious sphere will have to adapt. (Casanova 1994: 15)

This characterization of secularization enables us to understand what social theorists and sociologists of religion call "the theory of secularization." Actually, this is not a single theory but a collection of diverse theories, and there are a number of aspects that need to be carefully distinguished. The core of these theories concerns the functional differentiation of different secular spheres that emerge from processes of modernization, such as differentiation of state, economy, and science. The basic idea is that in the course of modern developments each of these spheres becomes differentiated and relatively autonomous, subject to its own procedures, norms, and regularities. A second aspect of theories of secularization is the decline of religion thesis. This is the claim that as the historical process of secularization develops, there is a decline of religion. Some proponents of these theories claim that religion will eventually disappear as the world becomes thoroughly secularized. A third aspect is that the public role of religion declines – religion is privatized. It becomes a matter of personal faith, and is removed from the public sphere.

Until recently theories of secularization (in all three aspects) were accepted virtually without question. But in the past few decades secularization theories have been severely criticized – especially the decline of religion thesis and the privatization thesis. Some sociologists of religion now advocate the complete abandonment of the theory of secularization. Religion is certainly not disappearing from the modern world. Indeed, the empirical evidence indicates a tremendous growth of a variety of different religions in many (although, not all) regions of the world. Furthermore, rather than increasing privatization, we find an almost aggressive move toward a public role for religion in social and political movements. This is what Casanova calls "deprivatization."

There is another ambiguity that has plagued theories of secularization. Presumably such theories have been advanced as descriptive and explanatory. And as social-scientific theories, they are subject to confirmation or refutation by empirical evidence. But in many formulations there is a clear normative bias. Implicitly or explicitly, it is affirmed that the decline and privatization of religion is a *desirable* goal. Many liberal political theorists draw on theories of secularization to advocate that religion ought to be privatized and ought not to play a role in the public political sphere.

Thus far I have been discussing the way in which scholars and social theorists discuss "secular" and "secularization." But there is a popular use of "secular" that is parasitic upon the theory of secularization. From the perspective of many religious believers, secularization is not a neutral social process. To the extent that secularization becomes the all-encompassing reality, it threatens the very existence of a religious way of life. That is why it has to be strongly opposed. From a Christian fundamentalist perspective, secularization is not the result of impersonal social forces; it is the conspiratorial aim of individuals and groups. Who are these nefarious agents? They are primarily the "secular humanists" – the godless, evil ones – who advocate sexual permissiveness, homosexuality, abortion, feminism, relativism, and atheism. They are unpatriotic, and they weaken the moral fiber of the country. As Steve Bruce tells us:

> The problem for both potential supporters and promoters of the new Christian right was to construct a cause of the many things which concerned them about their environment. The solution was 'secular humanism', which
>
> > Denies the deity of God, the inspiration of the Bible and the divinity of Jesus Christ.
> > Denies the existence of the soul, life after death, salvation and heaven, damnation and hell.
> > Denies the Biblical account of Creation.
> > Believes that there are no absolutes, no right, no wrong – that moral values are self-determined and situational. Do your own thing, 'as long as it does not harm anyone else'.
> > Believes in the removal of distinctive roles of male and female.

Believes in sexual freedom between consenting individuals, regardless of age, including premarital sex, homosexuality, lesbianism and incest.
Believes in the right to abortion, euthanasia (mercy killing), and suicide.
Believes in equal distribution of America's wealth to reduce poverty and bring about equality.
Believes in control of the environment, control of energy and its limitation.
Believes in the removal of American patriotism and the free enterprise system, disarmament, and the creation of a one-world socialistic government.
(Pro-Family Forum n.d.) (Bruce 1988: 77)

Anyone who holds *any* of the beliefs listed here is labeled a "secular humanist." These evil secular humanists are actively undermining conservative Christianity. It is difficult to see any coherence in this disparate list of "offenses" to Christian fundamentalism. Whatever purpose this list may serve in the ideological construction of the evil enemy, it doesn't really single out any well-defined group. There are many religious and nonreligious persons who hold some of these beliefs and make some of these denials. There is also the absurd consequence that any religious person who "doesn't believe in the divinity of Jesus Christ" is classified a "secular humanist."

Christian fundamentalists are extreme examples of the mentality that I have been criticizing. To deny absolutes, to question moral certainties, to depart from what they understand to be Christian "truths," is to be a "secular humanist." And for these fundamentalists, pragmatic fallibilism is just another version of "secular humanism." But even less extreme religious believers tend to think that pragmatic fallibilism is a form of atheistic secularism. I want to challenge this claim. I have already indicated that it is a serious (although all too common) mistake to think that pragmatic fallibilism is anti-religious and atheistic. Indeed, my more general thesis is that the mentalities that I have described can take (and have taken) both religious and nonreligious forms. There are religious and secular persons who claim absolute moral certainty and divide the world in rigid dichotomies. And there are religious and nonreligious persons committed to genuine fallibilism. This is why I have spoken about a clash of mentalities that cuts across the religious/secular divide.

The classical pragmatists actually *defended* religious faith. Their Christian background shaped many of their leading ideas. They argued that religious faith is not only compatible with pragmatic fallibilism but is actually *strengthened* by it. When William James introduced his popular conception of pragmatism in 1898, he declared: "There is no difference which doesn't make a difference, no difference in abstract truth which does not express itself in a difference of concrete fact, and of conduct consequent upon the fact, imposed on somebody, somehow, somewhere, and somewhen" (1977: 349). The very first example he gives to illustrate the pragmatic approach is the debate about God and materialism. He asks the question: "Is matter the producer of all things, or is a God there too?" Listen to what he says:

> Many of us, most of us, I think, now feel as if a terrible coldness and deadness would come over the world were we forced to believe that no informing spirit or purpose has to do with it, but it merely accidentally had come. The actually experienced details of fact might be the same on either hypothesis, some joyous; some rational, some odd and grotesque; but without God behind them, we think they would have something ghastly, they would tell no genuine story, there would be no speculation in those eyes that they do glare with. With God, on the other hand, they would grow solid, warm, and altogether full of real significance. (James 1977: 350)

Religious questions were always in the foreground of James's thinking. James, who suffered from bouts of melancholia throughout his life, tells us: "I have always thought that this experience of melancholia of mine had a religious bearing. I mean that the fear was so invasive and powerful that if I had not clung to scripture texts like 'The eternal God is my refuge,' etc., 'Come unto me, all ye that labor and are heavy laden,' etc., 'I am the resurrection and the life,' etc., I think I should have grown really insane" (James 1977: 7). James boldly defends "the right to believe." He declares: "Faith thus remains as one of the inalienable birthrights of our mind. Of course, it must remain a practical, not a dogmatic attitude. It must go with the toleration of other faiths, with the search for the most probable, and with the full consciousness of responsibilities and risks" (James 1977: 737). This is certainly a different type of faith than that professed by fundamentalists. It shuns dogmatism and absolute certainty. It is a faith infused with the pragmatic spirit.

Even Peirce, who is considered to be the most "tough-minded" and scientific of the pragmatists, proposed "a neglected argument for the reality of God." In a striking phrase, he declares: "As to God, open your eyes and your heart, which is a perceptive organ and you see him." Peirce integrated this religious outlook with his cosmological speculations. He elaborated a doctrine of "evolutionary love," which he based on a reading of the Gospels.

> Here then, is the issue. The Gospel of Christ says that progress comes from every individual merging his individuality in sympathy with his neighbors. On the other side, the conviction of the nineteenth century is that progress takes place by virtue of every individual's striving for himself with all his might and trampling his neighbor under foot whenever he gets a chance to do so. This may accurately be called the Gospel of Greed. Much is to be said on both sides.

I have not concealed, I could not conceal, my own passionate predilection. Such a confession will probably shock my
scientific brethren. (Peirce 1931–5: vi. 493)

John Dewey, who professed his faith in democracy, is
frequently taken to be the pragmatist who was most indifferent to religious concerns. But Bruce Kuklick (1985) has
shown that his Christian background shaped Dewey's most
fundamental ideas. Stephen Rockefeller (1991), in his
comprehensive study of Dewey's thought, argues for the
necessity of "approaching Dewey's thought from the perspective of its religious meaning and value" (p. x). In *A
Common Faith*, Dewey criticizes both "militant atheism"
and "supernaturalism." Consider Dewey's justification for
speaking of God and defending the religious dimension of
experience.

One reason why personally I think it fitting to use the word
"God" to denote the uniting of the ideal and the actual
which has been spoken of, lies in the fact that aggressive
atheism seems to me to have something in common with
traditional supernaturalism ... What I have in mind especially is the exclusive preoccupation of both militant atheism
and supernaturalism with man in isolation. For in spite of
supernaturalism's reference to something beyond nature, it
conceives of this earth as the moral centre of the universe
and man as the apex of the whole scheme of things. It
regards the drama of sin and redemption enacted within the
isolated and lonely soul of man as the one thing of ultimate
importance. Apart from man, nature is held to be accursed
or negligible. Militant atheism is also affected by lack of
natural piety ... The attitude taken is often that of man
living in an indifferent and hostile world and issuing blasts
of defiance. A religious attitude, however, needs the sense of
connection of man, in the way of dependence and support,
with the enveloping world that imagination feels is a universe. Use of the words "God" or "divine" to convey the

union of the actual with the ideal may protect man from a
sense of isolation and from consequent despair or defiance.
(Dewey 1986: 36)

These brief references to the classical pragmatists'
reflections on religious faith and experience are intended
to explode the caricature of pragmatism as a hostile, atheistic, secular humanism.[3] On the contrary, these thinkers
sought to articulate what they took to be vital in religious
faith and experience. Pragmatic fallibilism does not pose a
threat to religion, although it rejects all forms of uncritical
dogmatism. My primary objective, however, is not to
defend any specific pragmatic conception of religious
faith and experience. (There are striking differences and
conflicts among the classical pragmatist thinkers.) What I
want to emphasize is that *religious faith is deepened when a
fallibilistic spirit informs it.*

We must never underestimate the evil deeds that human
beings are capable of committing. And we cannot fully
anticipate the new forms of evil deeds that will arise. But
our task is to specify concretely what we mean when we
designate something as evil, and to clarify intelligent
responses to these evils. We should welcome and encour-
age serious debate about these vitally important issues.
We must avoid demonizing persons or thinking of evil as an
impersonal force operating in the world.

Religious fundamentalists are hostile and scornful of
pragmatically informed understandings of religion. But a
questioning, fallible attitude has a much greater claim to
being authentic to religious traditions than any form of
fundamentalism. Sometimes we forget how recently fundamentalism has emerged as a religious movement. There
is a tendency to merge together a number of very different
religious movements, but they ought to be carefully distinguished. The media today will speak of the New Christian

Right, evangelicals, and fundamentalists – as if they form a single monolithic group.

"Evangelicalism" describes a network of Protestant religious movements that arose in the eighteenth century. In a recent volume dedicated to the study of evangelicalism, the authors single out the following pattern of convictions to identify evangelicalism.

> Biblicalism (a reliance on the Bible as ultimate religious authority), conversionism (a stress on the New Birth), activism (an energetic, individualistic approach to religious duties and social involvement, and crucicentrism (a focus on Christ's redeeming work as the heart of essential Christianity). (Noll et al. 1994:6)

This schematic definition presents the key convictions of many evangelicals – although there are extremely varied interpretations of them. Not all evangelicals are committed to a *literal* reading of the Bible or to the *inerrancy* of the Bible. Furthermore, not all evangelicals are committed to a conservative political agenda. There have been evangelicals who have avoided any form of political involvement, and there have been evangelicals who have inspired and played important roles in some of the most progressive movements in the history of the United States. In the nineteenth century, evangelicals were leaders in anti-slavery movements, just as there were those, especially in the South, who defended slavery on Christian principles. In the early twentieth century there was a Social Gospel movement that joined forces with secular progressives in fighting for social and economic injustice. And evangelicals, especially Black evangelical churches, played a vital role in the Civil Rights movement of the 1960s. We do a great injustice to the diversity of the evangelical movement if we identify it with the Christian right. This is not to deny that there are many evangelicals today who vigorously support the conservative Christian right.

Fundamentalism in the USA is a reactive religious movement that has its origins in the last decades of the nineteenth century and the first decades of the twentieth century.[4] It started as a reaction against those liberal Protestants who sought to adapt Christian beliefs to the modern world and to modern science. Fundamentalism opposed the threat of Darwinism to the biblical story of creation. It rejected the higher biblical criticism that claimed that several different editors authored the Bible. More generally, fundamentalism was a reaction against the modern secular tide that seemed to threaten Christian faith and a Christian way of life.

The word "fundamentalism" has had an interesting semantic career. Today it has acquired a primarily negative connotation, but it did not begin as a term of abuse. It did not have its origins in the Old South, but rather in southern California. We can actually date the origin of the expression "fundamentalism" in the American context.

In 1910 Milton and Lyman Stewart, two devout Christian brothers who had made their fortune in the California oil business, embarked on a five-year programme of sponsorship for a series of pamphlets which were sent free of charge to 'English-speaking Protestant pastors, evangelists, missionaries, theological professors, theological students, YMCA secretaries, and editors of religious publications throughout the world'. Entitled *The Fundamentals: A Testimony of Truth*, the tracts, written by a number of leading conservative American and British theologians were aimed at stopping the erosion of what the brothers and their editors considered to be the 'fundamental' beliefs of Protestantism: the inerrancy of the Bible, the direct creation of the world, and humanity, *ex nihilo* by God (in contrast to Darwinian evolution): the authenticity of miracles, the virgin birth of Jesus, his Crucifixion and bodily resurrection; the substitutionary atonement (the doctrine that Christ died to redeem the sins of humanity); and (for some but not all believers) his imminent return to judge and rule over the world. (Ruthven 2004: 10–11)

The Stewart brothers were premillennial dispensationalists. They believed that the biblical prophecies about the "End Times," especially those in the Revelation of St John, were literally true, and that the Apocalypse was imminent. On the Day of Judgment, the saved would be divided from the damned, the godly from the ungodly, before the promised thousand-year reign of righteousness. (Other evangelical Christians believe that the Day of Judgment will follow the millennium, and hence are called post-millennialists.[5]) If the Apocalypse is imminent, then the duty of good Christians is to save as many sinners as possible, who will then be "raptured" into the presence of Christ on the Day of Judgment.

Three million copies of *The Fundamentals* were circulated, and in 1920 Curtis Lee Laws, a conservative Baptist editor, added the "ist" ending, and declared that "Fundamentalists were those ready to do battle for *The Fundamentals*" (Ruthven 2004: 12). Initially, fundamentalists expended more energy attacking liberal Protestants than in damning other sinners. Fundamentalists felt that the mainline urban Protestant churches disinherited them. Fundamentalism soon took root in rural communities, especially in the South and the Southwest. After the famous Scopes trial (1925) in Tennessee, which received extensive national attention, fundamentalists suffered a severe defeat in public opinion. Clarence Darrow, the brilliant, witty ACLU lawyer, humiliated the populist (and three times presidential candidate) William Jennings Bryan by exposing contradictions and absurdities in fundamentalist readings of the Bible. Even though the jury found Scopes guilty of breaking the state law that forbade any teaching that contradicted the biblical view of creation, the attempt to put evolution and modern science on trial backfired. "In the trial by public opinion and the press, it was clear that the twentieth century, the cities, and the universities had won a resounding victory, and that the country, the South, and the fundamentalists were guilty as charged" (Marsden 1980: 186). H. L. Mencken, the most famous journalist of the time, ridiculed and scorned the fundamentalists. Fundamentalists "retreated" to their own enclaves. They started their own publishing houses, radio stations, Bible schools, and seminaries. And their preaching focused on saving souls at home and establishing missionaries abroad while they awaited the Second Coming of Christ. There was a long period of latency when fundamentalism – although growing in numbers and strength – played little role in public political life.[6]

Fundamentalism came back into prominence in the late 1970s with a renewed and powerful vigor. The 1960s horrified fundamentalists. Student radicalism, anti-Vietnam War protests, the sexual revolution, and the beginnings of a feminist movement posed new threats to a Christian way of life. "Family values" were being called into question. And from a fundamentalist perspective, the courts, especially the Supreme Court, had become aggressive agents for spreading and enforcing secularism throughout the country. This was also a time when fundamentalists were becoming increasingly affluent and found many wealthy sympathizers willing to support their causes. Fundamentalism now appealed to a wider audience of Christians who were disturbed by secular challenges to a Christian way of life.[7]

The most significant event in the rise of the New Christian Right occurred in 1979 when Jerry Falwell, a popular fundamentalist Baptist preacher was persuaded to lead a new organization named the "Moral Majority." Prior to this, there had been a deep ambivalence about politics among fundamentalists (and there still is among most extreme apocalyptic fundamentalists). If the "End Times" are really imminent, then there is little point in dealing with the dirty world of politics. But politically conservative organizers saw a tremendous opportunity to organize fundamentalists and conservative evangelicals for national political purposes. Steve Bruce describes how they went about this.

> Concerns become social movements only when they are mobilized, and if we are looking for founders of the 'new' Christian Right, the best candidates would, surprisingly, be two Catholics and a Jew. Richard Viguerie, Paul Weyrich and Howard Phillips were three conservative activists who were responsible for planning and fund-raising behind a number of new conservative groups in the late 1960s and early 1970s. They believed that, beyond the common stock of economy and foreign policy, there were many socio-moral issues that could serve as the basis for an organized conservative movement. They were also innovators in seeking to build a movement that would be independent of the main parties and broader than such previous single-issue campaigns as the temperance crusades or the anti-Communist League of America. Although they quickly became a faction within the Republican Party, the New Christian Right began with ambitions to influence both major parties. (Bruce 2000: 71)

There is no doubt that organizing fundamentalists and conservative evangelicals was a brilliant political move by political conservatives. In the first month of it founding, the Moral Majority raised one million dollars. Six months after its founding, polls indicated that 40 percent of Americans had heard about the Moral Majority, and 80 percent in the

South and Southwest. In the first year of its organization, the Moral Majority claimed to have 300,000 members, including 70,000 ministers of religion.

In 1980, Jerry Falwell published *Listen America!*, a manifesto of the Moral Majority that was a call to arms to potential supporters and a public warning about its adversaries and evil enemies. The Moral Majority was intended to be a Judeo-Christian coalition that would include – in Falwell's words – "Catholics, Jews, Protestants, Mormons, Fundamentalists" (but, of course, not Muslims). Here are some choice quotes that give the flavor of this manifesto.

Experts estimate that between 5 million and 6 million babies have been murdered since January 22, 1973, when the U.S. Supreme Court, in a decision known as Roe v. Wade, granted women an absolute right to abortion on demand during the first two trimesters of pregnancy. (p.165)

Most Americans remain deeply committed to the idea of the family as a sacred institution. A minority of people in this country is trying to destroy what is most important to the majority. (p. 122)

Militant homosexuals march under the banner of "civil rights" or "human rights" ... demanding to be accepted as a legitimate minority. (p. 183)

It is our government that has attacked the family's role as a primary educator of children. (p. 131)

We are very quickly moving to an amoral society where nothing is either absolutely right or absolutely wrong. Our absolutes are disappearing. (p. 117)

Students are told that there are no absolutes and that they are to develop their own value systems. Humanists believe that ... moral values are relative, that ethics is situational. (p. 206)

The aim of the Moral Majority is to provide leadership in establishing an effective coalition who are (a) prolife, (b) profamily, (c) promoral, and (d) pro-American. (p. 259)

Right living must be re-established as an American way
of life ... The authority of Bible morality must once again
be recognized as the legitimate guiding principle of our
nation. (p. 265)[8]

It should be clear from these quotations (as well as the
earlier Pro-Family Forum statement) that fundamentalists
have been primarily concerned with domestic issues such
as abortion, homosexuality, gay marriage, family values,
and denial of prayer in schools. This is what the code term
"moral values" has come to mean. Patriotism and the
defense of the "American (Christian) way of life" have also
been central. Fundamentalists have always been anti-
Communist; they welcomed Reagan's characterization of
the Soviet Union as the "Evil Empire." But there had not
been much interest in foreign affairs and foreign policy – at
least until 9/11.

Perhaps the first great national political success of the
fundamentalists was the role they played in the election of
Ronald Reagan, although, ironically, it was Jimmy Carter
who was the born-again Christian, and Reagan didn't do
much to further the domestic agenda so dear to the fundamentalists. Political scientists and sociologists are still
debating whether the New Christian Right was a driving
force in the Reagan revolution or was simply riding on its
coattails. In 1988, Steve Bruce published a book with the
title, "The Rise and Fall of the New Christian Right." He
was perhaps a bit precipitous in his judgment. But in 1987
Falwell folded the Moral Majority. The bid of Pat
Robertson (the popular televangelist) for the Republican
nomination in 1988 ended in a miserable failure. Although
he spent more money than any other Republican candidate,
he failed to win a single primary. Polls showed that many
fundamentalists and conservative evangelical Protestants
did not like the overt mixing of politics and religion.

They preferred a secular politician who held some of the right positions rather than a televangelist. Bruce argues that the power and influence of the New Christian Right had been greatly exaggerated by both its enemies and its friends. "The NCR has failed to achieve any significant legislative success, it has failed in its main goal of Christianizing America, and there are few reasons to suppose that it will at some future time succeed ... what brought the NCR into being is so amorphous as to be barely identifiable while at the same time being irreversible: what troubles supporters of the NCR is modernity and it will not go away" (Bruce 1988: 182). Casanova echoes Bruce's cautionary warning when he writes: "A well-organized, vociferous minority, whose unexpected mobilization caught everybody by surprise but whose very loosely defined potential constituency never reached 20 percent of the population, had miraculously become, in the minds of many, a threatening majority" (Casanova 1994: 161).

But despite the failure of the first George Bush to win a second term and the political success of Bill Clinton – who personified what so many fundamentalists vehemently hated – the NCR did not go away. It was biding its time until another national opportunity would arise. That opportunity arose as a result of 9/11. The election of 2000 showed how closely the country was divided between the two major parties. Consequently, it became increasingly clear to Republican strategists that organizing sympathetic groups in key electoral states would be decisive in the 2004 election. Even before 9/11, Karl Rove, Bush's shrewd political advisor, was working on organizing the New Christian Right.[9] George W. Bush's pronouncements about abortion, gay marriage, and family values were just what the New Christian Right wanted to hear. The White House also made a number of key appointments of persons favored by conservative Christians.

There can be little doubt that 9/11 radically changed the mood of the country. And from that day on, Bush started – almost obsessively – using the language of evil, which struck deep chords among the New Christian Right. America in its "War on Terror" was fighting the great Satan, the Antichrist. In his study of the ethics of George W. Bush, Peter Singer points out that the clearest sign of the Christian evangelical influence on Bush is his repeated invocation of a conflict of good and evil.

> We have seen that Bush often talks of "the evil ones" and even occasionally of those who are "servants of evil." He urges us to "call evil by its name," to "fight evil," and he tells us that out of evil will come good. This language comes straight out of apocalyptic Christianity. To understand the context in which Bush uses this language, we need to remember that tens of millions of Americans hold an apocalyptic view of the world. According to a poll taken by *Time*, 53 percent of adult Americans "expect the imminent return of Jesus Christ, accompanied by the fulfillment of biblical prophecies concerning the cataclysmic destruction of all that is wicked." One of the signs of the apocalypse that will precede the Second Coming of Christ is the rise of the Antichrist, the ultimate enemy of Christ, who heads Satan's forces in the battle that will culminate in the triumph of the forces of God, and the creation of the Kingdom of God on Earth. Projecting this prophecy onto the world in which they live, many American Christians see their own nation as carrying out a divine mission. The nation's enemies therefore are demonized. That is exactly what Bush does. When during a discussion about the looming war with Iraq with Australian prime minister John Howard in February 2003, Bush said that liberty for the people of Iraq would not be a gift that the United States would provide, but rather, "God's gift to every human being in the world," he seemed to be suggesting that there was divine endorsement for a war to overthrow Saddam Hussein. David Frum, Bush's

speechwriter at the time of his "axis of evil" speech, says of Bush's use of the term "evil ones" for the people behind 9/11: "In a country where almost two-thirds of the population believes in the devil, Bush was identifying Osama bin Laden and his gang as literally satanic."

Frum has given an account of how Bush came to use the phrase "axis of evil" to refer to Iraq, Iran, and North Korea. In his initial draft, he compared America's enemies today with those in World War II, and referred to them as the "axis of hatred," but Michael Gerson, who had the overall responsibility for it and is an evangelical Christian, changed "hatred" to "evil" because he "wanted to use the theological language that Bush had made his own since September 11." (Singer 2004: 207–8)

Since 9/11, when Americans suddenly became painfully aware of their vulnerability to the terror of Islamic extremists, Bush's "theological language" has become extremely effective in arousing deep emotions and political support – not only among fundamentalists and conservative Christian evangelicals, but also among a larger Christian community. But, as Peter Singer notes, seeing the world as a grand battle between the forces of evil and the forces of good is not Christian orthodoxy, but rather what Christians once thought of as heresy.

Seeing the world as a conflict between the forces of good and the forces of evil is not, however, the orthodox Christian view, but one associated with the heresy of Manichaeanism. The Manichaeans were ferociously attacked by Augustine, who thought that seeing some kind of evil force as the source of all that is bad is a way of masking one's own failing. Centuries of suppression and frequent persecution, however, did not eradicate the Manichaean way of looking at the world. After the Reformation, the Manichaean view appeared in some Protestant sects and was brought by them to America, where it flourished ... Bush's readiness to see America as pure and good, and its enemies as wholly evil, has its roots in this American-Manichaean tradition. (Singer 2004: 209)

The one qualification I would add is that this is not quite what the Manichaeans professed. As I have previously indicated, this is really *quasi*-Manichaeanism –Manichaeanism with a Christian twist – because there is the underlying conviction that the forces of good will *triumph* over evil. God is on our side. This theological language is presented as if it is *the* religious or *the* Christian view. But it isn't; it is closer to what Christians once thought of as *heresy*.

Throughout history we have witnessed the cruelty and extreme violence of those who are absolutely certain that they know what is good and what is evil. Arthur M. Schlesinger, Jr., has recently declared that the great threat to civilization today is from religious fanatics.

> Religious fanaticism is the breeding place for the greatest current threat to civilization, which is terrorism. Most of the killing in the world – whether in Ireland, Kosovo, Israel, Palestine, Kashmir, Sri Lanka, Indonesia, the Philippines, Tibet – is the consequence of religious disagreement. There are no more dangerous people on earth than those who believe they are executing the will of the Almighty. It is this conviction that drives on terrorists to murder the infidel. (Schlesinger 2004: 116)

I agree with Schlesinger that "*there are no more dangerous people on earth than those who believe they are executing the will of the Almighty.*" That is why it is so disturbing and frightening when we hear something like this from our political leaders and fellow citizens, who think they are defending democracy and freedom. This is just the sort of uncritical absolutism that the pragmatic thinkers sought to root out and critique – the type of absolutism that corrupts democratic politics and religion.

Many Christians and other religious believers do *not* accept a view of the world as a grand conflict between the forces of evil and the forces of good. They also reject the idea of a clash of civilizations. They question the way in which Bush and his supporters use "evil" as a blanket term to justify dubious political policies. They are deeply suspicious of those who claim that they – and they alone – are the true believers who are executing the will of the Almighty. They believe that a fallibilistic spirit can and should inform their religious faith – whether they are Christians, Jews, Muslims, or followers of some other religion. When any individual, sect, or denomination presents itself as possessing the exclusive or definitive understanding of good and evil, when "evil" is used as a blanket term of condemnation to advance a dubious political agenda, then there is a *corruption* of religion. Religious believers and nonreligious persons should passionately oppose this invidious form of corruption.

Epilogue

What is to be Done?

I want to begin with a disclaimer. In the spirit of the pragmatic fallibilism that I have defended, it would be foolhardy
to offer grand solutions or blueprints to correct the abuse
of evil. Responsible choices and actions always demand
specificity, sensitivity to context, careful analysis, clarifica-
tion of real options, debate, and persuasion. But it doesn't
follow that there is nothing to be done. That would be a
counsel of despair. It is helpful to recall what Hannah
Arendt wrote in the preface to *The Origins of Totalitarianism*:
"This book has been written against a background of both
reckless optimism and reckless despair. It holds that
Progress and Doom are two sides of the same medal: that
both are articles of superstition, not of faith." It is also
helpful to recall Menand's thesis about how the lifelong
projects of Holmes, James, Peirce, and Dewey were creative
responses to the mentality that prevailed during the Civil
War – how they sought, and to a remarkable degree succeeded in fostering, a more open, flexible, experimental,
fallible mode of thinking and acting that helped to shape the
culture of political and everyday life in America. We are, of
course, living in radically different times. But, as I have
argued, the same or similar mentalities can take many
different historical forms. In times of widespread anxiety,
fear, and perceived crises, there arises a craving for

absolutes, firm moral certainties, and simplistic schemas that help make sense of confusing contingencies; they help to provide a sense of psychological security. Since 9/11 we have been living through such a time. Over and above the real dangers that we face, there has been a widespread sense of vulnerability from an enemy that is difficult to understand and locate. The "War on Terror" is unlike any other war in modern history. It is not a war against a sovereign state, a civil war, or even a guerilla war. We are fighting an amorphous and ambiguous enemy. It is not even clear how to conduct such a war or what would count as "victory." It is always unsettling and threatening when our conventional categories for making sense of the world break down, and when we are at a loss as to how to develop new, more appropriate tools for understanding what is happening. The careless talk of evil and the demonizing of our enemies do not help matters. On the contrary – as I have argued – they obscure complex issues, block inquiry, and stifle public debate about appropriate responses to an unsettling, fluid state of affairs. So what is to be done? Ordinary citizens must stand up to and oppose the political abuse of evil, challenge the misuse of absolutes, expose false and misleading claims to moral certainty, and argue that we cannot deal with the complexity of the issues we confront by appealing to – or imposing – simplistic dichotomies. There is a role for public intellectuals, educators, journalists, and artists to help guide the way – just as Holmes, James, Peirce, and Dewey did at a different time under radically different historical circumstances. There have been other moments in American history when the mentality that demonizes the enemy and divides the world into the forces of good and the forces of evil has prevailed. This was characteristic of the dark years of the McCarthy period. But McCarthyism was defeated, in part because there were those who had the courage to stand up and oppose McCarthy's demagoguery.

The problem is not just an American one. The clash of mentalities is in evidence throughout the world. Various forms of fundamentalism and fanaticism are spreading; they are becoming threatening mass movements. Earlier I argued that the mentality of pragmatic fallibilism is not *uniquely* American. Many citizens throughout the world share it. There is a new democratic cosmopolitanism that is beginning to emerge throughout the world – although it is still in its initial stages. Those who share a democratic faith that abhors the appeal to rigid ideologies must seek alliances with like-minded individuals throughout the world. There is also a lesson to be learned from Dewey and Arendt. Both teach us how *fragile* democracy really is – how its fate is always uncertain. There are no guarantees that it will persist and flourish. Democracy does *not* consist exclusively of elections and formal political institutions. There is a *democratic ethos* that must be kept alive. And this takes constant attention, work, and practice. The creation and sustenance of what Dewey called "creative democracy" is *always* a task before us. Robust fallibilism requires the cultivation of demanding democratic virtues and practices. There is always the danger that we will undermine this democratic ethos – and empty democracy of any substantive meaning.

We also need to rethink the role of religion in the contemporary world. Scholars have already begun to challenge various theories of secularization. This demands rethinking many of our conventional understandings of modernity. It also requires seeking to make sense of new phenomena, including the reasons why so many people throughout the world feel that religion supplies an important spiritual dimension to their lives, as well as the reasons for the appeal of militant forms of religious fundamentalism. We need to understand the "deprivatization" of religion and the ways in which religion has become a powerful force in social movements. We need to understand why and how religion has served emancipatory aims – as in the case of liberation theology in Latin America – and also served to foster terrorism. These are intellectual tasks, but there is also practical work to be done. It doesn't help to scorn, dismiss, or denigrate those who affirm their religious faith or to caricature all religion as if it were only ignorant superstition. Religion must not be identified with fundamentalism. But it is to be lamented that – especially in the United States – there has been a virtual collapse of progressive Christian public intellectuals. Reinhold Niebuhr had his disagreements with John Dewey, but they shared common ground in their social and democratic political vision. Niebuhr was a progressive Christian thinker and a liberal social reformer who exercised a powerful influence on both the Christian and the secular communities. The dominant voices of American Protestantism during the first half of the twentieth century were *not* those of fundamentalists, but rather of thinkers and activists committed to programs of social reform and social justice. They played a vital role in the Civil Rights movement during the 1960s. In Catholic circles there were also progressive thinkers and activists concerned with the plight of the poor and oppressed, such as Dorothy Day, Michael Harrington, and a group associated with the Catholic weekly, *Commonweal*. They read the Gospels as calling for the alleviation of the pain and suffering of the poor. The spirit of pragmatic fallibilism informed the religious faith of these Christian thinkers. But today there is simply no public liberal Christian thinker in America with the stature and influence of a Reinhold Niebuhr or a Michael Harrington. Fundamentalists and conservative televangelists are drowning out the voices of progressive, open-minded Christians. Religious thinkers, preachers, and pastors have a special responsibility to speak out against the abuse of evil – to show how it distorts and corrupts religious faith. They have a responsibility to remind their congregations and constituencies of the great religious tradition of faith seeking understanding, and to affirm that serious issues concerning the meaning of good and evil do not lend themselves to sloganeering and clever sound bites.

In sum, there is intellectual and practical work to be done to counter the abuse of evil and the mentality that it reflects. The time is ripe – indeed, it is urgent – for a revitalized, passionate commitment to furthering a genuine democratic faith that eschews the appeal to dogmatic absolutes and simplistic dichotomies; a democratic faith that fosters tangible public freedom where debate, persuasion, and reciprocal argumentation flourish; a democratic faith that has the courage to live with uncertainty, contingency, and ambiguity; a democratic faith that is thoroughly imbued with a fallibilistic spirit.

Notes

Introduction

1 Kant introduced the concept of "radical evil" into philosophy. For a discussion of what Kant meant by radical evil, see Bernstein 2002: ch. 1.
2 See also Giorgio Agamden's (1999) perceptive discussion of the *Muselmann*.
3 Christopher R. Browning sums up the judgment of many historians when he writes: "I consider Arendt's concept of the 'banality of evil' a very important insight for understanding many of the perpetrators of the Holocaust, but not Eichmann himself. Arendt was fooled by Eichmann's strategy of self-representation in part because there were so many perpetrators of the kind he was pretending to be" (2003: 3–4).

Chapter 1 The Clash of Mentalities: The Craving for Absolutes versus Pragmatic Fallibilism

1 See Putnam's (2002) critique of the fact/value dichotomy.
2 See Menand's discussion of the debates about cultural pluralism (2001: ch. 14). "Pluralisms."
3 I discuss the "myth of the framework" in my 1983, and "engaged pluralism" in the appendix, "Pragmatism and the Healing of Wounds," in my 1991.

Chapter 2 The Anticipations and Legacy of Pragmatic Fallibilism

1 See the exchange between Taylor and Habermas in Gutman 1994.
2 See Habermas's remarks about the influence of pragmatism on his thinking in the postscript to Aboulafia et la. 2002. Alan Ryan, in his illuminating study of John Dewey discusses the revival of a Deweyan style of philosophy. He claims that Taylor "is for the most part a Deweyean without knowing it" (Ryan 1995: 361). Taylor has written perceptively about William James. See his 2002 and also his essay "What is Pragmatism?" in Benhabib and Fraser 2004.
3 See Bernstein 1992 and Dickstein 1998.
4 The best-known contemporary philosopher to identify with the pragmatic tradition is Richard Rorty. He enjoys a wide readership among humanistic scholars, even though many "professional" analytic philosophers think he has abandoned "serious" rigorous thinking. But, unlike James, Holmes, and Dewey, he does not have the influence that they enjoyed among a much wider public.

Chapter 3 Moral Certainty and Passionate Commitment

1 For an account of Niebuhr's criticism of Dewey and Dewey's response, see Rice 1993; Westbrook 1991; and Diggins 1995. See also Cornel West's interview with Eduardo Mendieta (2004); and Sidney Hook, "The Moral Vision of Reinhold Niebuhr," in Hook 1974.
2 Two essays are especially relevant for understanding the pragmatic sense of tragedy and evil: the title essay, "Pragmatism and the Tragic Sense of Life" (1960), and "Intelligence and Evil in Human History" (1947).
3 In his article, "How Bush Really Won," Mark Danner analyzes Bush's speeches about the "War on Terror" during the presidential campaign: "In a few blunt lines Bush has

subsumed everything else beneath the preeminent shining banner of the war on terror, and subsumed that war beneath his own reputation for forthrightness, decisiveness, and strength. And he has identified uncertainty, hesitation, vacillation – even the sort of nitpicking that would seek to separate the war in Iraq from the war on terror – as not mistaken or foolish but dangerous. 'Relentless' ... 'Steadfast' ... 'Determined': these words came fast and strong, again and again. And then the climatic line: '*We will fight the terrorists across the globe so we do not have to fight them here at home!*" (2005: 50).

4 William James introduced the distinction between "the tough-minded" and "the tender-minded" into philosophical discussion. He claimed that pragmatism "can satisfy both kinds of demand." See "The Present Dilemma in Philosophy" in James 1977.

5 Arthur M. Schlesinger, Jr., stresses the importance of the distinction between a "preventive war" and a "preemptive war."

> Given the dispute attached to the idea of a "preventive" war, the Bush administration prefers to talk about "preemptive" war, and too many have followed its example. The distinction between "preemptive" and "preventive" is well worth preserving. It is the distinction between legality and illegality. "Preemptive" war refers to a direct, immediate, specific threat that must be crushed at once; in the words of the Department of Defense manual, "an attack initiated on the basis of incontrovertible evidence that an enemy attack is imminent." "Preventive" war refers to potential, future, therefore speculative threats. (Schlesinger 2004: 23).

The Iraqi war a preventive war, not a preemptive war.

6 Richard Rorty quotes these remarks by Isaiah Berlin in his 1989: 46. Despite some of my disagreements with Rorty's version of pragmatism, he is one of the most forceful and eloquent defenders of pragmatic fallibilism.

Chapter 4 Evil and the Corruption of Democratic Politics

1   Peter Singer observes that "Bush's tendency to see the world in terms of good and evil is especially striking. He has spoken about evil in 319 separate speeches, or about 30 percent of all the speeches he gave between the time he took office and June 16, 2003. In these speeches he uses the word 'evil' as a noun far more than he uses it as an adjective – 914 noun uses as against 182 adjectival uses. Only twenty-four times, in all these occasions on which Bush talks of evil, does he use it as an adjective to describe what people do – that is, to judge acts and deeds. This suggests that Bush is not thinking about evil deeds, or even evil people, nearly as often as he is thinking about evil as a thing, or a force, something that has real existence apart from the cruel, callous, brutal, and selfish acts of which human beings are capable" (2004:2).

2   My discussion of Arendt's conception of politics is based upon my earlier discussions of Arendt in my 1983 and 1996.

3   See my discussion of radical evil and the banality of evil in my 1996.

4   Arendt consistently used masculine nouns and pronouns when referring to human beings. But we should not forget that it is only relatively recently that women have been allowed to participate in political life.

5   See Arendt's discussion of power, strength, authority, and violence in "On Violence," in her 1972: 143ff. She describes power as follows: "Power corresponds to the human ability not just to act but to act in concert. Power is never the property of an individual; it belongs to a group and remains in existence only so long as the group keeps together. When we say of somebody that he is 'in power' we actually refer to his being empowered by a certain number of people to act in their name. The moment the group, from which the power originated to begin with (*potestas in populo*, without a people or group there is no power) disappears, 'his power' also vanishes."

6   I have been stressing the overlap between Arendt and the pragmatic conception of democratic politics, especially in regard to

what they perceive as the danger of introducing absolute good and evil into politics. But there are also some striking differences. Arendt thought that the type of politics she describes is limited to the few – to a political elite – although she insisted that *everyone* ought to have the opportunity to enter into the political sphere. This is why she preferred – as did the Founding Fathers – to speak about the Republic. The checks and balances of republican government were intended to prevent the excesses of unrestrained democracy. Dewey had a much greater faith in the "common man," and the potential of *all* individuals to participate in democratic politics. Furthermore, Dewey would never accept the sharp distinction that Arendt draws between "the social" and "the political." For a critique of Arendt's distinction, see my article, "Rethinking the Social and the Political," in my 1986.

7 In his press conference on Sept. 16, 2001, President Bush said: "This is a new kind of – a new kind of evil. And the American people are beginning to understand. This crusade, this war on terrorism is going to take a while." Muslims around the world were incensed with this reference to a "crusade." Bush soon stopped speaking about a "crusade" against evil and terrorism.

8 When Schmitt speaks of "liberalism," he is not using the expression as it is commonly used today in the United States, as the name of a political orientation that is distinguished from and opposed to "conservatism." Rather, he is referring to the classical doctrine of liberalism that emphasizes individual rights and the alleged neutrality of the state in the protection of these rights. Liberalism in this sense has its roots in the philosophy of John Locke (although Schmitt thinks that it can be traced back to Hobbes). The United States is Schmitt's preeminent example of liberal society in the twentieth century – and the target of his harshest criticism.

9 Schmitt insists on enmity as the basic human (political) condition, but rarely seeks to justify this claim. Heinrich Meier, one of the most insightful German scholars of Schmitt, persuasively argues that Schmitt's understanding of "the

political" is rooted in his *political theology*. Meier also provides
a perceptive analysis of the changes in the several editions of
The Concept of the Political, which he interprets as responses in
hidden dialogue with Leo Strauss. See Meier 1995 and 1998.
For an analysis of Schmitt that challenges some of Meier's
claims, see Scheuerman. See also McCormick 1997.

10 There are right and left Schmittians. There are those who
(selectively) appeal to Schmitt to explain and "justify" the
"War on Terror," and those who (selectively) appeal to
Schmitt to condemn the "War on Terror" as a disastrous total
war "justified" by hypocritical universal moral principles of
good and evil. For differing accounts of the use of Schmitt by
the right and the left, see Lilla 1997 and Wolfe 2004.

Chapter 5 Evil and the Corruption of Religion

1 See Danner 2004. See also Steinfels 2004. Steinfels points
out that "when Pope John Paul II weighed in on the question
[of intrinsic evil] in his 1993 encyclical 'The Splendor of
Truth,' the list of . . . actions he described as evil 'in themselves, independently of circumstances' included, along with
genocide and slavery, 'physical and mental torture.'"

2 Andrew Sullivan wrote this shortly before Alberto R. Gonzales
was confirmed by the Senate to be the US Attorney-General
by a vote of 60 (for) to 36 (against). Recently, there has been
new evidence that foreign governments working secretly with
the United States have been torturing prisoners captured by
the Americans. This "outsourcing" of torture elicited a strong
editorial from *The New York Times*. "What is going on here is
not what supporters of the administration's policies depict:
an awful but necessary and skilled inquiry reserved for the
worst terrorists, who hold secrets that could cost innocent
lives. . . . This is about a system that was hastily conceived,
ineptly formulated, incompetently administered and now out
of control. It lowers the humanity of the people who practice
it, and the citizens who condone it ("Self-Inflicted Wounds,"
The New York Times, Feb. 15, 2005, A15).

3 See also the articles collected in Rosenbaum 2003, including my essay, "Pragmatism's Common Faith." See Stout 2004 for an illuminating and passionate defense of a pragmatic understanding of religion and democracy.

4 I am restricting my discussion to Protestant religious fundamentalism in the USA. Although the term originated in the USA, it is used today to identify a variety of religious movements, including Islamic fundamentalism. The most comprehensive study of fundamentalism in the world today is *The Fundamentalism Project*, a series of five volumes edited by Martin E. Marty and R. Scott Appleby and published by the University of Chicago Press. Sponsored by the American Academy of Arts and Sciences, these five volumes contain articles by an international group of leading religious scholars. For briefer studies of fundamentalism, see Bruce 2000, and Ruthven 2004.

5 Steve Bruce notes that there is a link between these two polar positions and the prevailing social climate. "In times of social crisis and economic depression, the more pessimistic premillennialist view tends to dominate. In periods of social optimism, such as that enjoyed by the USA in the first two decades of the twentieth century, the postmillennialist view tends to be more attractive" (Bruce 2000: 11).

6 José Casanova notes that during the Great Depression, "Evangelical Protestantism had ceased being a public civic religion . . . Along with the economy, religion was undergoing it own 'depression.' After the war, both religion and the economy underwent a typical cyclical revival, and the 'Christianization' of the American people continued apace, but the character of Christianity had changed. Religion had become increasingly privatized, and Protestantism had become just another denomination. The Protestant churches and other denominations could, and often did, still enter the public sphere. But they were no longer established there. They had to compete not only among themselves but, most important, with secular rivals" (Casanova 1994: 143).

7 Some commentators such as Martin E. Marty think that Protestant fundamentalism has now "peaked," and that other

Protestant groups such as the Pentecostals are rapidly growing in the USA and throughout the world.

8 See José Casanova's illuminating analysis of *Listen, America!* (Casanova 1994: 150–4).

9 The New Christian Right includes more than Protestant conservative evangelicals and fundamentalists. It also includes a significant number of Catholic conservatives, who share many of the same domestic concerns as conservative Protestants, e.g. about abortion, homosexuality, single-sex marriage. The political significance of this Christian coalition is illustrated by what happened in Ohio in the 2004 presidential election. Ohio is a state that had suffered an economic downturn and extensive unemployment, and many pundits thought Kerry had a good chance of winning there. If John Kerry had received an additional 60,000 votes, he would have won Ohio's twenty electoral votes and the national election. But the coalition of conservative Protestants and Catholics was largely responsible for Bush's victory in Ohio. In addition to the conservative evangelical vote, Bush received 55 percent of the Catholic vote.

Works Cited

Aboulafia, Mitchell, Bookman, Myra, and Kemp, Catherine (eds) 2002: *Habermas and Pragmatism*, New York: Routledge.

Agamben, Giorgio 1999: *Remnants of Auschwitz: The Witness and the Archive*, tr. Daniel Heller-Roazen. New York: Zone Books.

Arendt, Hannah 1958: *The Human Condition*. Chicago: University of Chicago Press.

—— 1963: *On Revolution*. New York: Viking Press.

—— 1965: *Eichmann in Jerusalem: A Report on the Banality of Evil*, 2nd edn. New York: Viking Press.

—— 1968: *The Origins of Totalitarianism*, 3rd edn, rev. New York: Harcourt Brace Jovanovich.

—— 1971: Thinking and Moral Considerations: A Lecture. *Social Research*, 38/3.

—— 1972: *Crises of the Republic*. New York: Harcourt Brace Jovanovich.

—— 1977a: *Between Past and Future*. New York: Penguin Books.

—— 1977b: *The Life of the Mind: Thinking*, vol.1. New York: Harcourt Brace Jovanovich.

—— 1994: *Essays in Understanding*, ed. Jerome Kohn. New York: Harcourt Brace & Co.

Arendt, Hannah, and Jaspers, Karl 1992: *Correspondence 1926–1969*, ed. Lotte Kohler and Hans Saner, tr. Robert and Rita Kimber. New York: Harcourt Brace & Co.

Benhabib, Seyla, and Fraser, Nancy (eds) 2004: *Pragmatism, Critique, Judgment: Essays for Richard J. Bernstein*. Cambridge, Mass.: MIT Press.

Berlin, Isaiah 1969: *Four Essays on Liberty.* Oxford: Oxford University Press.

Bernstein, Richard J. 1983: *Beyond Objectivism and Relativism: Science, Hermeneutics, and Praxis.* Oxford: Basil Blackwell.

——1986: *Philosophical Profiles.* Philadelphia: University of Pennsylvania Press.

——1991: *The New Constellation: The Ethical-Political Horizons of Modernity/Postmodernity.* Cambridge: Polity.

——1992: The Resurgence of Pragmatism, *Social Research,* 59 (Winter).

——1996: *Hannah Arendt and the Jewish Question.* Cambridge: Polity.

——2002: *Radical Evil: A Philosophical Interrogation.* Cambridge: Polity.

Browning, Christopher R. 2003: *Collected Memories: Holocaust History and Postwar Testimony.* Madison: University of Wisconsin Press.

Bruce, Steve 1988: *The Rise and Fall of the New Christian Right.* Oxford: Oxford University Press.

——2000: *Fundamentalism.* Cambridge: Polity.

Casanova, José 1994: *Public Religions in the Modern World.* Chicago: University of Chicago Press.

Commission 2004: *The 9/11 Commission Report,* authorized edition. New York: W. W. Norton.

Danner, Mark 2004: *Torture and Truth.* New York: New York Review of Books.

——2005: How Bush Really Won. *New York Review of Books,* 52/1 (January 13).

Dewey, John 1927: *The Public and its Problems.* New York: Henry Holt.

——1930: *Individualism: Old and New.* New York: Minton, Balch.

——1981: *The Philosophy of John Dewey,* ed. John J. McDermott. Chicago: University of Chicago Press.

——1986: *A Common Faith* (1934). In *The Later Works of John Dewey* 1925–53, vol. 9, ed. Jo Ann Boydston. Carbondale: Southern Illinois Press.

——1988: Creative Democracy: The Task Before Us (1939). In *The*

Later Works, 1925–53, vol. 14, ed. Jo Ann Boydston. Carbondale: Southern Illinois University Press.

Dickstein, Morris (ed.)1998: *The Revival of Pragmatism*. Durham, NC: Duke University Press.

Diggins, Jack Patrick 1995: *The Promise of Pragmatism*. Chicago: University of Chicago Press.

Gutman, Amy (ed.) 1994: *Multiculturalism,* expanded paperback edition. Princeton: Princeton University Press.

Hook, Sidney 1974: *Pragmatism and the Tragic Sense of Life*. New York: Basic Books.

James, William 1977: *The Writings of William James,* ed. John McDermott. Chicago: University of Chicago Press.

Kant, Immanuel 1960: *Religion within the Limits of Reason Alone,* tr. T. M. Greene and H. H. Hudson. New York: Harper Torchbooks.

Kuklick, Bruce 1985: *Churchmen and Philosophers: From Jonathan Edwards to John Dewey.* New Haven: Yale University Press

Levi, Primo 1986: *Survival in Auschwitz* and *The Reawakening: Two Memoirs,* tr. Stuart Woolf. New York: Summit Books.

Lilla, Mark 1997: The Enemy of Liberalism. *New York Review of Books,* 44/8 (May 15).

MacIntyre, Alasdair 1977: Epistemological Crises, Dramatic Narrative and the Philosophy of Science. *Monist,* 60.

McCormick, John P. 1997: *Carl Schmitt's Critique of Liberalism: Against Politics as Technology.* Cambridge: Cambridge University Press.

Marsden, George M. 1980: *Fundamentalism and American Culture: The Shaping of Twentieth Century Evangelicalism, 1870–1925.* New York: Oxford University Press.

Meier, Heinrich 1995: *Carl Schmitt and Leo Strauss: The Hidden Dialogue,* tr. J. Harvey Lomax. Chicago: University of Chicago Press.

—— 1998: *The Lesson of Carl Schmitt: Four Chapters on the Distinction between Political Theology and Political Philosophy,* tr. Marcus Brainard. Chicago: University of Chicago Press.

Menand, Louis 2001: *The Metaphysical Club: A Story of Ideas in America.* New York: Farrar, Straus and Giroux.

Neiman, Susan 2004: *Evil in Modern Thought: An Alternative History of Philosophy,* with a new preface for the paperback edition. Princeton: Princeton University Press.

Noll, Mark A., Bebbington, David W., and Rawlyk, A. (eds)1994: *Evangelicalism: Comparative Studies of Popular Protestantism in North America, the British Isles, and Beyond, 1700–1990*. New York: Oxford University Press.

Peirce, Charles S. 1931–5: *Collected Papers of Charles Sanders Peirce*, ed. Charles Hartshorne and Paul Weiss. Cambridge, Mass. Harvard University Press.

——1992: *The Essential Peirce*, vol. 1, ed. Nathan Houser and Christian Kloesel. Bloomington, Ind.: Indiana University Press.

Power, Samantha 2004: Hannah Arendt's Lesson. *New York Review of Books,* 51/7 (April 29).

Putnam, Hilary 1994: *Words and Life*, ed. James Conant. Cambridge, Mass.: Harvard University Press.

——2002: *The Collapse of the Fact/Value Dichotomy and Other Essays*. Cambridge, Mass.: Harvard University Press.

Rice, Daniel F. 1993: *Reinhold Niebuhr and John Dewey: An American Odyssey*. Albany, NY: SUNY Press.

Rockefeller, Steven 1991: *John Dewey: Religious Faith and Democratic Humanism*. New York: Columbia University Press.

Rorty, Richard 1989: *Contingency, irony, and solidarity*. Cambridge: Cambridge University Press.

Rosenbaum, Stuart (ed.) 2003: *Pragmatism and Religion*. Urbana: University of Illinois Press.

Ruthven, Malise 2004: *Fundamentalism: The Search for Meaning*. Oxford: Oxford University Press.

Ryan, Alan 1995: *John Dewey and the High Tide of American Liberalism*. New York: W. W. Norton.

Scheuerman, William E. 1999: *Carl Schmitt: The End of Law*. New York: Rowman & Littlefield.

——2004: International Law as Historical Myth. *Constellations,* 11/4.

Schlesinger, Arthur M., Jr. 2004: *War and the American Presidency*. New York: W. W. Norton.

Schmitt, Carl 1995: *The Concept of the Political,* tr. with intro. by George Schwab, with a new foreword by Tracy B. Strong. Chicago: University of Chicago Press.

Sellars, Wilfrid 1963: *Science, Perception and Reality*. New York: Humanities Press.

——1997: *Empiricism and the Philosophy of Mind*, with an intro.

by Richard Rorty and a commentary by Robert Brandom. Cambridge, Mass.: Harvard University Press.

Singer, Peter 2004: *The President of Good & Evil: The Ethics of George W. Bush.* New York: Dutton.

Steinfels, Peter 2004, The Ethical Questions involving Torture of Prisoners are Lost in the Debate over War in Iraq. *The New York Times,* Dec. 4.

Stout, Jeffrey 2004: *Democracy & Tradition.* Princeton: Princeton University Press.

Sullivan, Andrew 2005: Atrocities in Plain Sight. *New York Times Book Review,* Jan. 23.

Suskind, Ron 2004: Without a Doubt. *New York Times Magazine,* Oct. 17.

Taylor, Charles 2002: *Varieties of Religion Today: William James Revisited.* Cambridge, Mass.: Harvard University Press.

West, Cornel 1989: *The American Evasion of Philosophy.* Madison: University of Wisconsin Press.

——2004: Empire, Pragmatism, and War: An Interview with Eduardo Mendieta. *Logos,* 3/3 (Summer).

Westbrook, Robert B. 1991: *John Dewey and American Democracy.* Ithaca, NY: Cornell University Press.

Wolfe, Alan 2004: A Fascist Philosopher Helps us to Understand Contemporary Politics. *The Chronicle Review,* April 2.

Index

Index

DATE DUE
